65

QUESTIONS

and

ANSWERS

about

PATRIARCHAL

BLESSINGS

65 QUESTIONS *and* ANSWERS *about* PATRIARCHAL BLESSINGS

ALONZO L. GASKILL

CFI

An imprint of Cedar Fort, Inc.

Springville, Utah

ISBN 13: 978-1-4621-2171-7

Published by CFI, an imprint of Cedar Fort, Inc.
2373 W. 700 S., Springville, UT 84663
Distributed by Cedar Fort, Inc., www.cedarfort.com

LIBRARY OF CONGRESS CATALOGING-IN-PUBLICATION DATA

Names: Gaskill, Alonzo L., author.
Title: 65 questions and answers about patriarchal blessings / Alonzo L.
  Gaskill.
Other titles: Sixty-five questions and answers about patriarchal blessings
Description: Springville, UT : CFI, An imprint of Cedar Fort, Inc., [2017] |
  Includes bibliographical references and index.
Identifiers: LCCN 2017056417 (print) | LCCN 2017058582 (ebook) | ISBN
  9781462128693 (epub, pdf, mobi) | ISBN 9781462121717 | ISBN
  9781462121717 (perfect bound : alk. paper)
Subjects: LCSH: Patriarchal blessings (Mormon Church) | Church of Jesus
  Christ of Latter-day Saints--Doctrines. | Mormon Church--Doctrines.
Classification: LCC BX8643.P36 (ebook) | LCC BX8643.P36 G37 2017 (print) |
  DDC 264/.093320992--dc23
LC record available at https://lccn.loc.gov/2017056417

Cover design by Shawnda T. Craig
Cover design © 2018 Cedar Fort, Inc.
Edited and typeset by McKell Parsons and Kaitlin Barwick

Printed in the United States of America

10 9 8 7 6 5 4 3 2 1

Printed on acid-free paper

In memory of Verdell L. Nyland (1919–2002)
—Stake Patriarch—
Whose prophecy regarding my life has
blessed me for more than three decades.

— CONTENTS —

PREPARING FOR YOUR PATRIARCHAL BLESSING

ONCE YOU HAVE RECEIVED YOUR PATRIARCHAL BLESSING

—ACKNOWLEDGMENTS—

I WISH TO EXPRESS MY SINCERE APPRECIATIONS TO THE NUMEROUS stake patriarchs who took time out of their very busy schedules to read drafts of this manuscript (during both its formative and summative stages) and to offer their insights and experiences. Their suggestions were most helpful, and the final manuscript is greatly improved because of the counsel these good and consecrated men offered.

In addition, I express my undying appreciation to Jan Nyholm, who provided a formative edit of this manuscript. The American novelist and satirist, Kurt Vonnegut Jr., wrote, "The Universe needs more good editors, God knows." In the case of my writing, that is so very true. As this book attests, we were all foreordained (in the premortal world) to certain mortal missions. I think one of Jan's foreordained life missions was to come to earth to fix my poorly written books. I am eternally indebted.

—INTRODUCTION—

When I was investigating The Church of Jesus Christ of Latter-day Saints during my college years, one of the things that drew me to it was its teaching that there are living prophets and apostles upon the earth today; men who are capable, because of their ordination, of receiving modern revelation on behalf of God's latter-day Church and kingdom. Consequently, I was absolutely enamored with the Doctrine and Covenants and its 138 revelations received by those ordained as prophets, seers, and revelators.

When, some months after my conversion, I learned about the office of stake patriarch—and the ability of faithful members to receive a patriarchal blessing, or personal revelation from God—I was ecstatic. I simply could not wait to receive my own blessing from the Lord.

Nearly eleven months after I was baptized, I had the good fortune of visiting the stake patriarch for the Independence Missouri Stake of Zion—Brother Verdell L. Nyland. As he and I sat alone in his living room, he placed his hands upon my head and, as a patriarch in Zion, pronounced upon me my patriarchal blessing.

As a new member of the Church—young and immature in the gospel—I had hoped that my blessing would make extravagant promises and would declare that I was from some obscure and exotic lineage. However, my blessing was quite normal, and certainly not "extravagant" in its content. Of course, it had what struck me as some nice promises and some wise warnings, but nothing seemingly dramatic.

However, as the years have passed since I received my patriarchal blessing—and as I've thoughtfully studied it, while gaining a bit of life experience—I've realized how remarkably detailed the blessing is and how absolutely prophetic it is. Because I was young and immature at the time I received it, I couldn't understand many of the things spoken of in my blessing. However, as I've aged and lived through the fulfillment of many of the promises made therein, I am *absolutely convinced* that the stake patriarch had the gift of prophecy and the spirit of revelation. I am in awe at how accurately he described my future, my gifts, and many of my life's experiences.

I had never met Brother Nyland prior to that day, and I never saw him again after he gave me my blessing. However, nearly two decades after receiving my patriarchal blessing, I coincidentally ran into a woman from the Independence Missouri Stake. I asked her if the patriarch was still alive, and she informed me that he was—and that he was living in Utah. She gave me his address, and I wrote him a short letter to express my gratitude for my blessing and to bear witness that I knew he had been inspired on that day when he laid his hands upon my head and pronounced my patriarchal blessing. Much to my sorrow, I later learned that my letter arrived only days after Brother Nyland had passed away.

Now, more than thirty years after the patriarch blessed me—and having lived to see *so many* of God's promises to me fulfilled—I have been asked to put together this little book on patriarchal blessings. I am grateful for the opportunity to write this, if for no other reason than to bear testimony to the world that God has given us a wonderful and miraculous gift in our patriarchal blessings, a gift that perhaps many of us have not quite caught the vision of. Therefore, as I dedicate this work to the memory of Verdell L. Nyland—an inspired patriarch and man of God—I encourage each of you to dedicate yourselves to a more sincere study of your patriarchal blessing, that you might gain a deeper testimony of God's hand in your life, and that you might more fully understand your sacred mortal mission.

What Is a
Patriarchal Blessing?

———

–1–

What Is a Patriarchal Blessing?

THIS MAY BE ONE OF THE MOST IMPORTANT QUESTIONS ANSWERED in this book. After all, if you do not understand the significance of a patriarchal blessing, you may not see the need to get one; and even if you *do* choose to receive your blessing, if you don't understand why it is so significant, you may not use it as the Lord intended.

The First Presidency of the Church has explained, "Patriarchal blessings contemplate an inspired declaration of the lineage of the recipient, and also, where so moved upon by the Spirit, an inspired and prophetic statement of the life mission of the recipient, together with such blessings, cautions, and admonitions as the patriarch may be prompted to give for the accomplishment of such life's mission."[1] In other words, your patriarchal blessing is a revelation from God to you, which will tell you a bit about your past (i.e., what tribe you have come from) and also a little about your future (i.e., what your mortal mission is). It is "a personal revelation from God"[2] in which you will be promised certain blessings but also warned of things that could rob you of those blessings.

Your blessing may mention certain responsibilities you will be given in life. It may speak of gifts of the Spirit that God intends to endow you with. It will certainly promise you great blessings—contingent upon your faithfulness. Many patriarchal blessings will refer to life events, such as a mission, marriage, or callings. Patriarchal blessings often offer warnings and admonitions that will help you with potential challenges you may have in life. Occasionally, patriarchal blessings will warn of certain weaknesses we have that might threaten our salvation. Thus, one reason to regularly read your blessing is so that you can avoid these dangers or pitfalls.

As a "personal revelation" from your Heavenly Father,[3] your patriarchal blessing is "your own 'personal scripture.' "[4] It "is like having your very own section of the Doctrine and Covenants—a revelation especially for you."[5] Think of the significance of that. Most human beings will *never* have the chance to have a personal passage of scripture given *just to them*. Yet Heavenly Father has offered *you* exactly that. Thus, your patriarchal blessing is a most sacred gift—one to be cherished and read regularly. President James E. Faust (1920–2007), who served as a member of the First Presidency, explained, "A priesthood blessing is sacred. . . . If, through our priesthood blessings, we could perceive only a small part of the person God intends us to be, we would lose our fear and never doubt again."[6]

President Thomas S. Monson (1927–2018), sixteenth President of the Church, explained that your blessing "literally contains chapters from your book of eternal possibilities."[7] It will tell you about many of the things that can happen and many of the blessings that will be given to you, *if* you live faithful to your covenants. President Monson called patriarchal blessings "a Liahona of light to guide you unerringly to your heavenly home."[8] In other words, just as the Liahona was a "small" thing which brought about "great things" (1 Nephi 16:29)—but only according to the "faith and diligence" one gave it (1 Nephi 16:28–29)—so also, your patriarchal blessing may seem like a small thing (only a page or two in length), but it can bring about great things (by protecting you and guiding you) if you have faith in it, and if you are diligent in obeying its counsel to you.[9] Like the Liahona, which guided Nephi and his family to the promised land, your patriarchal blessing can guide you to the celestial kingdom.[10]

One of the ways in which a patriarchal blessing can help you on your journey is by pointing out dangers along the way. Heavenly Father knows you better than you know yourself. He knows your strengths, but He also knows your weaknesses—and He knows that *Satan knows your weaknesses too*. Therefore, Father in Heaven has given you many helps in your attempt to make it back to His presence: the Holy Ghost, the teachings of living prophets, priesthood leaders, inspired parents and teachers, and personal prayer.

In addition to all of these, God has also given us patriarchal blessings. Your blessing can serve as a shield and a protection for you against the powers of Satan.[11] Jesus knows every strategy the devil is going to use against you. Your patriarchal blessing will point out to you those strategies and where you have weaknesses so that—if you follow the counsel of your blessing—Satan will not be able to destroy you.[12] Those of us who supported Heavenly Father's plan in the premortal existence (see Abraham 3:26)—and who have come here to mortality—are at war with Satan. Our patriarchal blessing should be part of our battle plan to defeat the "enemy of all righteousness" (Acts 13:10).[13]

In addition to protecting you from spiritual and even physical danger, your blessing can keep you pointed in the right direction—and keep you on target to accomplish the many marvelous things God wants you to accomplish in your life. It can help you to figure out what your personal life mission is and how to accomplish that. In addition, it can also lift you up during your most difficult times. President James E. Faust (1920–2007) suggested, "Our blessings can encourage us when we are discouraged, strengthen us when we are fearful, comfort us when we sorrow, give us courage when we are filled with anxiety, and lift us up when we are weak in spirit. Our testimonies can be strengthened every time we read our patriarchal blessings."[14]

Your blessing is a sacred and unique gift to you from God. No one has a blessing just like yours because no one's needs are exactly like yours. Your patriarchal blessing will tell you exactly what you need to know in order to be exalted. While it isn't a commandment to receive a patriarchal blessing,[15] *you need one!* We all do. If regularly read and contemplated, your blessing will be one of the greatest helps you could ever have in overcoming temptation, figuring out your life's profession, finding your eternal companion, enduring your trials, and returning home to your Father and Mother in Heaven.

Notes

1. First Presidency letter to stake presidents, 28 June 1957, cited in Bruce R. McConkie, *Mormon Doctrine*, 2nd ed. (Salt Lake City, UT: Bookcraft, 1979), 558.
2. James E. Faust, "Priesthood Blessings," *Ensign*, November 1995, 81–82.
3. See Faust, "Priesthood Blessings," 81–82.
4. Julie B. Beck, "You Have a Noble Birthright," *Ensign*, May 2006, 107.
5. Ed J. Pinegar and Richard J. Allen, *Your Patriarchal Blessing* (American Fork, UT: Covenant Communications, 2005), 6; John L. Lund, *Understanding Your Patriarchal Blessing* (Orem, UT: Noble Publishing, 1980), 8.
6. Faust, "Priesthood Blessings," 80.
7. Thomas S. Monson, "Your Patriarchal Blessing: A Liahona of Light," *Ensign*, November 1986, 66.
8. Monson, "Your Patriarchal Blessing," 67.
9. See Pinegar and Allen, *Your Patriarchal Blessing*, 8–9; Garry H. Boyle, *A Loving Letter from God: Your Patriarchal Blessing* (Springville, UT: Cedar Fort, 2015), 44–45.
10. See Boyle, *A Loving Letter from God*, 44.
11. See Boyd K. Packer, "The Stake Patriarch," *Ensign*, November 2002, 42.
12. Ezra Taft Benson, "In His Steps," Brigham Young University devotional, March 4, 1979, 2.
13. See Boyle, *A Loving Letter from God*, 80.
14. Faust, "Priesthood Blessings," 83.
15. See Spencer W. Kimball, *The Teachings of Spencer W. Kimball*, Edward L. Kimball, comp. (Salt Lake City, UT: Bookcraft, 1998), 505.

—2—

When Was the First
Patriarchal Blessing Given?

THE WORD *PATRIARCH* IS A LATIN WORD, AND HAS TWO PARTS: *PATRI*, meaning "father," and *arch*, meaning "chief." Thus, the word *patriarch* means quite literally "chief father."[1] The words *father* and *patriarch* are, therefore, synonyms.

That being said, technically, the first patriarchal blessing was most likely given by our Heavenly Father (the "Chief Patriarch") in the premortal existence prior to each of us leaving His presence to come here to mortality. One stake patriarch explained, "Your [patriarchal] blessing is a prophetic synopsis with excerpts of the blessing you received at Heavenly Father's hand as you prepared to come to earth."[2] In blessing you, the stake patriarch only says what God tells him to, but the blessing is *not* from the patriarch; it is from God, our eternal Patriarch. The stake patriarch's responsibility is simply to reveal to you bits and pieces of the Father's blessing you received before you left your heavenly parents to come here to mortality. Thus, the first patriarchal blessing would be the one God the Eternal Father gave to each of His children before they left His presence.

The first patriarchal blessings here in mortality would be the ones Adam gave his posterity after the Fall. In addition to the many blessings that he likely pronounced upon his posterity over his nearly one thousand years of life, three years prior to his death, he blessed each of his children with a patriarchal blessing. Doctrine and Covenants 107:41 states that the patriarchal order "was instituted in the days of Adam." The prophet Joseph taught,

"I saw Adam in the valley of Adam-ondi-Ahman. He called together his children and blessed them with a patriarchal blessing. The Lord appeared in their midst, and he (Adam) blessed them all, and foretold what should befall them to the latest generation. This is why Adam blessed his posterity; he wanted to bring them into the presence of God."[3] From the time of the Fall, righteous fathers—who are the natural patriarchs to their posterity—have given inspired patriarchal blessings to their posterity. This began with Adam, and has continued down through the line of faithful fathers until our day.

In Genesis 48–49, the patriarch Jacob—also known as Israel—gave a patriarchal blessing to each of his twelve sons and to two of his grandsons. It is through these descendants of Jacob that we each trace our patriarchal lineage, the lineage that is revealed to us when our stake patriarch lays his hands upon our head and pronounces upon us our patriarchal blessing.

In this dispensation, Joseph Smith Sr. (father to the prophet Joseph) was the first ordained patriarch, though his son (Joseph Smith Jr.) gave the first patriarchal blessings in these latter days.[4] Joseph Sr. was ordained Patriarch to the Church on December 18, 1833, by his son, Joseph Jr., with the assistance of Oliver Cowdery, Sidney Rigdon, and Fredrick G. Williams. Prior to Joseph Smith Sr.'s call and ordination as the Church's patriarch, his son—the prophet Joseph—gave patriarchal blessings to members of the Church. The first of those patriarchal blessings in this dispensation were given on December 18, 1855, to the prophet's mother and siblings.[5]

Notes

1. See *Patriarchal Blessings* (Salt Lake City, UT: The Church of Jesus Christ of Latter-day Saints, 1979), 2.
2. Garry H. Boyle, *A Loving Letter from God: Your Patriarchal Blessing* (Springville, UT: Cedar Fort, 2015), 50.
3. Joseph Smith, *Teachings of the Prophet Joseph Smith*, Joseph Fielding Smith, comp. (Salt Lake City, UT: Deseret Book, 1976), 158–159.

4. R. Clayton Brough and Thomas W. Grassley, *Understanding Patriarchal Blessings* (Springville, UT: Horizon Publishers, 2008), 13.

5. See H. Michael Marquardt, *Early Patriarchal Blessings of The Church of Jesus Christ of Latter-day Saints* (Salt Lake City, UT: The Smith-Pettit Foundation, 2007), 4–7.

—3—

What Makes a Patriarchal Blessing Different from Other Priesthood Blessings I've Received?

YOU WILL RECEIVE MANY, MANY BLESSINGS OVER THE COURSE OF your life: a baby blessing shortly after you were born; a confirmation blessing after you were baptized; setting apart blessings for callings; blessings for health, comfort, or direction; etc. However, your patriarchal blessing is unique from each of those in three significant ways.

First of all, your patriarchal blessing will be the only blessing you will ever receive from someone who has been ordained to an office in the priesthood that has as its only function and calling to receive revelation for other people. In other words, I may get a blessing from my father, or from my bishop, or from my home teacher— and, in so doing, each of those men would act in the authority of the Melchizedek Priesthood. However, none of those men has as his sole function (as father, bishop, or home teacher) the ability to receive revelation for people who come to them. However, a stake patriarch is ordained to that office in the Melchizedek Priesthood for that very reason, and for that reason alone. Thus, his blessing of you is by calling and ordination and not by relationship (as it is with your bishop, father, or home teacher).

A second way in which your patriarchal blessing is different from other blessings you might receive in life is this: a patriarchal blessing is the only priesthood blessing you will ever get that will be recorded—word for word—and preserved in the archives of the Church. While we record on the records of the Church that various ordinances have been performed—including ordinances that typically have a blessing associated with them (like your confirmation or priesthood ordination)—nevertheless, we do not preserve on the records of the Church the word-for-word blessing given. Yet, with a patriarchal blessing, this is exactly what we do, setting it apart from other priesthood blessings you might receive.

Finally, your patriarchal blessing is different from other blessings you will receive in that it is the only priesthood blessing that is designed to declare your lineage, specifying which of the tribes of Israel your blessings will be received through. Indeed, one official Church publication pointed out that the declaration of one's lineage is the "most important part of your blessing."[1] That cannot be said of any other priesthood blessing you will receive.

Note

1. See *Patriarchal Blessings* (Salt Lake City, UT: The Church of Jesus Christ of Latter-day Saints, 1979), 2.

—4—

Who Can Receive a Patriarchal Blessing?

ALL WORTHY, ACCOUNTABLE MEMBERS OF THE CHURCH OF JESUS Christ of Latter-day Saints can *and should* receive a patriarchal blessing. The Lord has specific promises and blessings in reserve for each of His children. Your blessing is a means of learning about some of those, and it will give you inspired guidance on how to lay hold of those promises and blessings.

While a person who is not a member of the LDS Church may receive a priesthood blessing from someone holding the Melchizedek Priesthood (if they desire one, and if they are willing to exercise faith in God's restored priesthood power), nevertheless, they are not authorized to receive a patriarchal blessing because they have not yet entered into the covenants by which one becomes a member of the house of Israel.

—5—

Should a Person Who Has a Severe Intellectual Disability Receive a Patriarchal Blessing?

THE CHURCH HANDBOOK OF INSTRUCTIONS STATES, "EVERY worthy, baptized member is entitled to and should receive a patriarchal blessing."[1] If one is accountable enough to be baptized, then he or she should receive a blessing from an ordained stake patriarch. However, if—because of an intellectual disability—the member's bishop does not believe he or she is accountable, then there is no benefit in that person receiving a patriarchal blessing. The Handbook notes, "Each patriarchal blessing is sacred, confidential, and personal."[2] The blessing is to be interpreted (under the influence of the Spirit) *only* by the person who received the blessing. If a member would not be able to interpret his or her blessing, then it is not appropriate for the blessing to be given in order for someone else—such as a parent—to try to interpret it.

Understandably, sometimes parents of children with intellectual disabilities wish for the child to have a patriarchal blessing because the parents feel that the blessing will give them greater insight into who their child is or into who he or she was in the premortal existence. Some feel that it will help them to have a greater sense of their child's eternal destiny. While it is commendable that parents wish to know these things, a patriarchal blessing is not the way for them to gain such knowledge. Members of the Church should keep in mind that a patriarchal blessing is for the recipient of the blessing, and not for the parents of the recipient.[3] Consequently, if parents wish to understand such details about their son or daughter who has special needs, they should seek personal revelation on these matters through earnest prayer and fasting, or perhaps through a priesthood blessing given by the disabled child's father, grandfather, or bishop.

Though we do not traditionally give a patriarchal blessing to those who are developmentally disabled to the degree that they are unable to understand what a patriarchal blessing is, nevertheless, it should be understood that God still has profound blessings in store for them—and an important mission for them. However, He will reveal those blessings and that mission in a way that they can understand and experience. Knowing that a patriarchal blessing is for the recipient—and for him or her alone—we should not pressure priesthood leaders to give a patriarchal blessing to those who do not need or cannot (in mortality) use one.

Notes

1. *Handbook 2: Stake Administering the Church* (Salt Lake City, UT: Intellectual Reserve, Inc., 2010), 20.12.1.
2. *Handbook 2*, 20.12.2.
3. See *Handbook 1: Stake Presidents and Bishops* (Salt Lake City, UT: Intellectual Reserve, Inc., 2010), 16.12.1.

—6—

How Is a Patriarchal Blessing Given?

ON THE DAY OF YOUR BLESSING, JUST PRIOR TO LAYING HIS HANDS upon you, the patriarch will typically spend a few minutes talking informally with you. This is not a worthiness interview. (Your bishop will interview you for worthiness prior to issuing you a recommend to receive a patriarchal blessing.) Rather, your informal conversation with the patriarch prior to receiving your blessing is intended to accomplish a couple of things. It gives the patriarch a chance to get a feel for you and your spirit. It also provides him with an opportunity to instruct you regarding patriarchal blessings and to let you know what is about to happen. It can also serve to help you to get comfortable with him prior to receiving your blessing.

As with any other blessing, the patriarch will seat you in a chair in front of him and place his hands upon your head in order to confer the blessing. The symbolism inherent in this act is important for you to understand. One author explained, "In the performance of his role, . . . the patriarch himself is a symbol of God's beneficence. The one symbolic gesture he employs in bestowing blessings is the laying on of hands, which signifies God's will and power channeled directly through the patriarch to the blessing recipient."[1] The laying on of hands traditionally symbolizes that "the recipient [of the blessing] has been touched by the hand of God, conveying the idea of transmission of power from on high (D&C 36:2)."[2] The ordained patriarch does not simply operate under God's authority but actually in concert with God. If worthy, there is a oneness that is to exist between the patriarch and God, who speaks to and through him during the act of the laying on of hands. As he gives you your blessing, the patriarch symbolizes God—because it is the Father that is blessing you, not the patriarch. As an illustration of this idea, note the language used in most priesthood blessings. The person giving the blessing may state, "By the authority of the Melchizedek Priesthood" (which indicates what priesthood he is operating under), but he may also add, "In the name of Jesus Christ" (suggesting that the words to be spoken are not his own but, rather, are Christ's words and Christ's will).

> The priesthood holder acts in Christ's stead, doing the things the Lord would do if he were here. In that process, the priesthood holder is an agent and representative of the Savior himself. This truth is underscored in a principle the Lord expressed to Edward Partridge: "I will lay my hand upon you by the hand of my servant Sidney Rigdon . . . " (D&C 36:2). The Lord did not actually place his hands upon Edward Partridge's head. Instead, he commissioned Sidney Rigdon. . . . In the process, though, it was truly as though the Lord himself were laying his hands upon Brother Partridge's head. . . . Priesthood holders are . . . types or shadows of the great High Priest.[3]

Thus, the patriarch is simply a surrogate—a stand-in—for God the Father and His Son, Jesus Christ. His hands upon you are God's hands, and his words spoken to you are God's words.

Notes

1. Gary Shepherd and Gordon Shepherd, *Binding Earth and Heaven: Patriarchal Blessings in the Prophetic Development of Early Mormonism* (University Park, PA: Pennsylvania State University Press, 2012), 55.
2. Donald W. Parry and Jay A. Parry, *Symbols & Shadows: Unlocking a Deeper Understanding of the Atonement* (Salt Lake City, UT: Deseret Book, 2009), 12.
3. Parry and Parry, *Symbols & Shadows*, 8–9.

—7—

Is There a Structure or Format That Patriarchal Blessings Generally Follow?

PATRIARCHAL BLESSINGS TRADITIONALLY HAVE FOUR GENERAL SEC-
tions, though some blessings will vary in this regard.[1]

The first section is the heading, which includes genealogical
information such as your name, your parents' names, your place and
date of birth, the patriarch's name, etc. (The patriarch won't state all
of this information during the actual blessing, but it will appear at
the top of your blessing when you receive your typed copy of your
patriarchal blessing.) Just as the declaration of your lineage is an
important part of a patriarchal blessing, this information portion of
your blessing serves to connect you to your ancestors. Because this
blessing will become part of the Church's permanent records, this
brief bit of genealogy helps to ensure that the record of your blessing
is properly archived.

The second section of your blessing will be a sort of introduc-
tion, where the patriarch will state your full name and also the
authority by which he is pronouncing your blessing. A patriarchal
blessing is a priesthood blessing. Thus, it is traditionally the practice
that the authority of the patriarch is stated—usually in this section,
but sometimes also near the end of the blessing.

The third section is the main body of the blessing, wherein the
patriarch declares your lineage and promises various blessings and
gifts, along with cautions, admonitions, and warnings, as the Spirit
dictates. This is traditionally the longest portion of the blessing and
the part you'll most likely spend the rest of your life seeking to
understand and watching to be fulfilled.

Finally, the last section of your blessing is usually where the patriarch might offer what are sometimes referred to as the "sealing blessings." These are promises that—if you are faithful—you will come forth in the morning of the first Resurrection or that you will dwell with your spouse or preside over your posterity throughout eternity. Those blessings are "sealed" upon you, as with all blessings, contingent upon your faithfulness.[2] "There are few places where the word *seal* is used in connection with a blessing of the priesthood. A patriarchal blessing is one of those places where it may be used. . . . To seal is to make the blessings, promises, and gifts binding forever. It solemnizes, authenticates, and makes them a protective element in your life."[3] Of course, if this "sealing" is not mentioned in your blessing, it does not imply that the promises made will not come to pass.

Notes

1. R. Clayton Brough and Thomas W. Grassley, *Understanding Patriarchal Blessings* (Springville, UT: Horizon Publishers, 2008), 53.
2. John A. Widtsoe, *Evidences and Reconciliations*, vol. 1 (Salt Lake City, UT: Bookcraft, 1943), 74.
3. Garry H. Boyle, *A Loving Letter from God: Your Patriarchal Blessing* (Springville, UT: Cedar Fort, 2015), 57.

—8—

What Portions of My Life Can My Patriarchal Blessing Address?

YOUR PATRIARCHAL BLESSING COULD POTENTIALLY DISCUSS ANY aspect of your life: your strengths, relationships, callings, health, weaknesses, etc. However, it will likely not cover *all* of these. Indeed, many patriarchal blessings don't mention some of the things that happen in most of our lives, such as marriage or the rearing of children. One patriarch suggested that the things mentioned in most blessings are not the mundane or typical life occurrences but, instead, "the outstanding things which might happen."[1]

Some people are frustrated that their blessing doesn't give as much detail as they would like or that their blessing mentions a gift or caution but doesn't go into any detail regarding it. One stake patriarch suggested, "God wants you to have plenty of opportunities to use your gift of agency to learn from your choices and experiences."[2] Thus, Heavenly Father is not going to tell you every little detail—thereby limiting your choices. God "wants to inspire, not script, your life."[3] President Ezra Taft Benson (1899–1994), thirteenth President of the Church, explained, "Usually the Lord gives us the overall objectives to be accomplished and some guidelines to follow, but he expects us to work out most of the details and methods."[4] Some patriarchal blessings are surprisingly specific ("vocationally, the Lord would have you be a teacher") and others more vague ("you will work with young people"). If you feel like your blessing is more general than it is specific, take that as evidence that God trusts you to use your agency to make wise and righteous choices without needing to be "command[ed] in all things" (D&C 58:26).[5]

Of the gifts or talents mentioned in most of our patriarchal blessings, Elder Bruce R. McConkie (1915–1985), of the Quorum of the Twelve Apostles, explained:

> When we pass from preexistence to mortality, we bring with us the traits and talents there developed. True, we forget what went before because we are here being tested, but the capacities and abilities that then were ours are yet resident within us [in mortality]. Mozart is still a musician [as he was in the premortal existence]; Einstein retains his mathematical abilities; Michelangelo his artistic talent; Abraham Moses, and the prophets their spiritual talents and abilities. Cain still lies and schemes. And all men with their infinitely varied talents and personalities pick up the course of progression where they left it off when they left the heavenly realms.[6]

Elder McConkie added, "All men, and the servants of the Lord in particular, acquired, in [the] preexistence, by obedience to law, the specific talents and capacities with which they are endowed in this life."[7] This being the case, any time your patriarchal blessing mentions one of your talents or gifts, it is discussing who you were in the premortal world.

Finally, President Harold B. Lee (1899–1973), who was the eleventh President of the Church, explained, "What we have received here in this earth [life] was given to each of us according to the merits of our conduct before we came here."[8] In other words, many of the promises made to you in your patriarchal blessing have been made because you earned the right to those promises because of your faithfulness when you dwelt in your Father in Heaven's presence. The fact that you were born with access to the restored gospel is a direct result of your obedience in the premortal existence. The fact that you are inclined to believe in God and His prophets is a direct result of the faith you developed in the premortal world. The fact that you are told in your patriarchal blessing that you will have certain gifts of the Spirit manifest in your life here in mortality is a direct result of your spirituality prior to your birth. Those who were faithful there, will be rewarded here; and many of those earned blessings—if we can appropriately call them "earned"—will be mentioned in your patriarchal blessing.

Notes

1. Eldred G. Smith, "What is a Patriarchal Blessing?" *The Instructor* 97, no. 2 (February 1962): 43.
2. Garry H. Boyle, *A Loving Letter from God: Your Patriarchal Blessing* (Springville, UT: Cedar Fort, 2015), 8.
3. Boyle, *A Loving Letter from God*, 15.
4. Ezra Taft Benson, *God, Family, Country: Our Three Great Loyalties* (Salt Lake City, UT: Deseret Book, 1974), 152.
5. See Boyle, *A Loving Letter from God*, 74.
6. Bruce R. McConkie, *The Mortal Messiah*, 4 vols. (Salt Lake City, UT: Deseret Book, 1979–1981), 1:23, 25.
7. McConkie, *The Mortal Messiah*, 3:470.
8. Harold B. Lee, "Understanding Who We Are Brings Self-Respect," *Ensign*, January 1974, 5.

—9—

Will My Patriarchal Blessing Speak about Every Major Life Event?

IN AN OFFICIAL PUBLICATION OF THE CHURCH ON PATRIARCHAL blessings, it states, "The Lord does not intend to solve all of our problems for us."[1] Nor is he going to list in our blessing every potential temptation, gift, relationship or accomplishment we might have. Your blessing is but a sampling of some of the most important of these. As President James E. Faust (1920–2007) of the First Presidency explained, "A person should not expect the blessing to detail all that will happen to him or her or to answer all questions. The fact that one's patriarchal blessing may not mention an important event in life, such as a mission or marriage, does not mean that it will not happen."[2]

Similarly, you should keep in mind that your blessing may mention events in your life but not discuss them in chronological order. For example, I knew a young man who went on a full-time mission. Shortly after he arrived in his assigned field of labor, he reread his patriarchal blessing. It suddenly struck him that near the beginning of his blessing it talked about how he would marry in the temple, but it wasn't until near the end of his blessing that it mentioned that he would serve a full-time mission. The young missionary assumed that his patriarchal blessing was listing these events in the order in which they would happen, so the elder packed his bags and went home—certain that he was not supposed to serve a mission until after he had married. By erroneously assuming that each promise mentioned in a patriarchal blessing is given in chronological order, this young elder robbed himself of the blessings of serving a full-time mission and robbed others of the opportunity to hear the gospel from his lips. (If he weren't supposed to serve at nineteen years old, the prophet would not have called him on a mission at nineteen years old.)

Your patriarchal blessing will give you hints of things to come, warnings about things to avoid, promises of blessings available, and gifts to equip you to fulfill your life's mission. Nevertheless, many of your life's events will go unmentioned in your blessing.[3] That being said, if you heed the counsel and warnings in your blessing, it will help you in just about every circumstance you find yourself in. One stake patriarch suggested, your blessing will be "a catalyst, a lightning rod for new revelation. When you ponder on your patriarchal blessing, you show respect and interest in knowing God's will. This will tune you into God and open the channel to receive more revelations concerning your life, important decisions, and your future."[4] Thus, while your patriarchal blessing will not speak about *every* aspect of your life, it can be a springboard for revelation on *every part* of your life. Of course, this will require that you read it regularly and prayerfully contemplate the things discussed therein.

Notes

1. *Patriarchal Blessings* (Salt Lake City, UT: The Church of Jesus Christ of Latter-day Saints, 1979), 2.
2. James E. Faust, "Priesthood Blessings," *Ensign*, November 1995, 82.
3. See Eldred G. Smith, "What Is a Patriarchal Blessing?" *The Instructor* 97, no. 2 (February 1962): 43.
4. Garry H. Boyle, *A Loving Letter from God: Your Patriarchal Blessing* (Springville, UT: Cedar Fort, 2015), 111.

–10–

Do the Promises in My Patriarchal Blessing Pertain Only to This Life?

WHILE A SIGNIFICANT PERCENTAGE OF THE PROMISES MADE TO YOU in your patriarchal blessing will be fulfilled in mortality—provided you remain faithful—nevertheless, some of the promises mentioned may not be fulfilled during this life but may come to pass in the post-mortal spirit world or in the Resurrection. Patriarchal blessings can (and often do) discuss events from one's pre-mortal life, their mortal probation, and also their post-mortal existence.[1] Elder John A. Widtsoe (1872–1952) of the Quorum of the Twelve Apostles wrote, "It should always be kept in mind that the realization of the promises made may come in this [life] or the future life."[2] The fact that many patriarchal blessings end with a promise that the recipient will "come forth in the morning of the first Resurrection" suggests that most—if not all—patriarchal blessings have *at least part* of their fulfillment in the next life. President Thomas S. Monson (1927–2018) has said, "What may not come to fulfillment in this life may occur in the next. We do not govern God's timetable."[3] Each of us should read our patriarchal blessing with an eternal perspective in mind. One book of patriarchal blessings reminds us, "You may have cultivated . . . whatever qualities, attributes, and talents you might find mentioned in your patriarchal blessing . . . for a long while *before* you came to this earth. In a way, you might be on a journey to rediscover them and apply them for good in serving the needs of your family and others while in this phase of your life."[4]

Elder Eldred G. Smith (1907–2013), the last general Patriarch to the Church, cautioned that we not assume that the patriarch has spoken in error if someone dies before all of their blessing has been fulfilled. Elder Smith explained:

> Now, some people say, "So and so was given such and such in his blessing and he died before it was ever fulfilled." Well, so what? That isn't the end of his life or the end of what can be accomplished as the result of mortality. The purpose of mortality or what we can accomplish here is between birth and the Resurrection. So many things which we should accomplish in this life and don't get the opportunity to accomplish may be accomplished after death, but before the Resurrection.[5]

Our individual eternal missions are much larger than could be accomplished in the short span of a mortal lifetime. Indeed, they are as "broad as eternity."[6] Thus, some of the promises made in your blessing may not be fulfilled in this life. Some may be accomplished in the postmortal spirit world, others potentially in the Millennium, and still others during the Resurrection. That is by divine design!

Notes

1. See *Patriarchal Blessings* (Salt Lake City, UT: The Church of Jesus Christ of Latter-day Saints, 1979), 2.
2. John A. Widtsoe, *Evidences and Reconciliations*, vol. 1 (Salt Lake City, UT: Bookcraft, 1943), 75.
3. Thomas S. Monson, "Your Patriarchal Blessing: A Liahona of Light," *Ensign*, November 1986, 66.
4. Ed J. Pinegar and Richard J. Allen, *Your Patriarchal Blessing* (American Fork, UT: Covenant Communications, 2005), 59–60.
5. Eldred G. Smith, "Patriarchal Blessings," address given at the Salt Lake Institute of Religion, January 17, 1964, 5.
6. See Garry H. Boyle, *A Loving Letter from God: Your Patriarchal Blessing* (Springville, UT: Cedar Fort, 2015), 43–44. See also 154–55.

–11–

What If Some of the Promises Made in My Blessing Are Not Fulfilled?

IN SOME WAYS, THIS QUESTION IS RELATED TO THE PREVIOUS QUESTION. However, there are a couple of other things to consider here as it relates to unfulfilled promises.

Knowing that the ordained patriarchs in the Church are inspired of God, there are only three reasons why the promises in someone's blessing would not be fulfilled.

First—*and most concerning*—is one's personal worthiness. If, indeed, some promise made was not fulfilled, or some blessing offered was never received, it may be because the person did not live worthy of the things the Lord had promised him or her. If we do not strive to live faithful to our covenants, then we may miss opportunities to receive the blessings promised to us. As a singular example, if a young man's patriarchal blessing says that he will serve a full-time mission *in his youth*, and will thereby be the instrument in bringing many souls into the restored gospel, but then he is not worthy to serve a mission as a young man, that opportunity (and the associated blessings) would be lost or, at the very least, delayed. He can certainly repent and serve a senior mission. However, if he was not worthy during the time the blessing was to be received, he would simply miss out on that promise made in his blessing.

A second reason why some promises in a patriarchal blessing might *appear* to go unfulfilled has to do with timing. In other words, it may simply not be time for that element in the blessing to be fulfilled. President Boyd K. Packer (1924–2015), former president of the Quorum of the Twelve Apostles, explained:

> Sometimes someone will worry because a promise made in a patriarchal blessing is not yet fulfilled. For instance, a blessing may indicate that a member will be married, and they do not find a companion. That does not mean that the blessing will go unfulfilled. It is well to know that *things happen in the Lord's due time*, not always in ours. Things of an eternal nature have no boundaries. From the premortal existence to our existence beyond the veils of death, our life is an eternal life.[1]

As a singular example, if a young woman's blessing promises her that she will be sealed to her eternal companion in the holy temple and, at fifty years old, she finds herself still single, that should not be taken as evidence that this promise will not be fulfilled. The Lord will bring to pass His promises according to His timing and in His way. Elder Neal A. Maxwell (1926–2004) of the Quorum of the Twelve Apostles suggested the importance of being willing to say not only, "Thy will be done, O Lord," but "Thy timing be done" as well.[2]

Finally, some assume that certain promises in their patriarchal blessing were uninspired because they have not witnessed their fulfillment in their lives (see Hebrews 11:13). However, in many cases, the promised blessing *has* been fulfilled, but not in the way it was expected. Thus, sometimes we don't notice their fulfillment and assume that either the patriarch was wrong or that God has let us down. As an example, Elder LeGrand Richards of the Twelve Apostles told of the death of his oldest son—who was not quite sixteen years of age when he passed. In the boy's patriarchal blessing, it promised, "For it will be thy privilege to bear the holy Priesthood and to go even among strangers and in strange lands, in defense of truth and righteousness." He was also told in his blessing that "thy home shall be a fit abode for the spirits of thy loved ones." Elder Richards and his wife had interpreted these promises as meaning that their son would serve a mission to some country where he would likely learn a foreign language; and that, upon his return, he would marry and have children. Thus, when the boy died, Elder Richards and his wife were devastated and confused. It was one of their younger children that pointed out to them that his older brother *was* currently serving a mission among "strangers and in a strange land."

Additionally, the younger brother noted that his brother's new home *was* a "fit abode for the spirits of his loved ones."[3] Similarly, my patriarchal blessing promised me the gift of tongues. My immediate assumption was that I would be serving a foreign-speaking mission. However, I was called on an English-speaking mission to England. I have absolutely experienced the gift of tongues in my life, but it has been in a very different way than I assumed the Lord meant (when He promised me this gift in my blessing). Had I not changed my paradigm, the fulfillment of that promise in my life might well have gone unnoticed.

Notes

1. Boyd K. Packer, "The Stake Patriarch," *Ensign*, November 2002, 45; emphasis added.
2. Neal A. Maxwell, "Plow in Hope," *Ensign*, May 2001, 59.
3. Legrand Richards, in Conference Report, October 6, 1939, 25–26.

—12—

Can Promises in My Blessing Be Fulfilled through My Posterity Instead of through Me?

MANY YEARS AGO, A DEAR FRIEND APPROACHED ME, CONCERNED that certain blessings made in her husband's patriarchal blessing appeared to have gone unfulfilled. She asked if there was any way that these promises could be fulfilled through one of their children—as it didn't look likely that they could now be fulfilled directly through her husband's life.

In response to this same concern, Patriarch to the Church Eldred G. Smith (1907–2013) taught this: "Some of the interpretations" of our patriarchal blessings "may be fulfilled by our descendants. We are now in a large part fulfilling some of the outstanding blessings given to the children of Israel by their father. We may not realize all of the blessings in our lifetime. They may be fulfilled after our death or by our descendants." Elder Smith added, some of our blessings will be "realized in different ways from what we expect. But as long as we live worthy of our blessings, we have an anchor upon the promise of the Lord that they will be fulfilled."[1]

As an illustration, President James E. Faust (1920–2007) spoke of a promise made to his father (George A. Faust) in his patriarchal blessing. This promise was *not* fulfilled directly through George, nor through Elder Faust and his four brothers. Rather, it was fulfilled through George's posterity, starting with his grandchildren.[2] Certainly, George Faust's life choices made it possible for his grandchildren to fulfill the promise; and, had he made other choices, he could have prevented his grandchildren from fulfilling what God had foretold. Nevertheless, Brother Faust was faithful, and the promises made to him came to fruition in the lives of his posterity. Such may be the case for some of us, and the blessings the Lord has promised us in our individual patriarchal blessings.

Notes

1. Eldred G. Smith, "What Is a Patriarchal Blessing?" *The Instructor* 97, no. 2 (February 1963): 43.
2. James E. Faust, "Priesthood Blessings," *Ensign*, November 1995, 83.

−13−

How Many Patriarchal Blessings Can I Receive from a Stake Patriarch?

IN THE EARLY DAYS OF THE RESTORATION, IT WAS FAIRLY COMMON for people to request and receive multiple patriarchal blessings. In part, this practice may have grown out of a lack of understanding (by the lay members of the Church) as to the nature and purpose of patriarchal blessings.

Today, within the Church, we are counseled to get just one patriarchal blessing—to declare our lineage. Then, if we need additional guidance, we should go to our fathers (as our natural patriarchs) or to other worthy priesthood holders who have stewardship for us (such as a husband, bishop, stake president, elder's quorum president, or home teacher) for additional blessings.[1] Rarely would a second blessing from a stake patriarch be approved; and rarely would one actually be necessary.[2]

Elder Eldred G. Smith (1907–2013), who served as the last general Patriarch to the Church, explained:

> People want to know why it is recommended that only one patriarchal blessing be given by an ordained patriarch. When an ordained patriarch has given a blessing with all the requirements of the declaration of lineage and the sealing blessings and it is on record—recorded in the Church archives—then it is superfluous to keep repeating that same thing over again and putting it on record. It just fills up space in the Historian's Office unnecessarily.[3]

Elder Smith's point is that a new blessing is not likely to tell you additional things. In support of this, one source suggested that those who have somehow been able to get a second blessing "report that it 'said the same thing' as the original blessing. . . . Rather than requesting another blessing, concerned members [should] prayerfully work to understand the one they have."[4]

As we will discuss later in this book (see Question 54), if there are things that bother you about the content of your patriarchal blessing, you should go to the Lord in prayer and ask Him to reveal to you a *correct* understanding of those items of concern. If you feel something was left out of your blessing, you can go to your father or grandfather (as your natural patriarchs) and have them give you a priesthood blessing to address those specific things you feel you need a patriarchal revelation on.

In rare circumstances, there may have been things (such as family or emotional issues) at the time the original blessing was given—or something mentioned in the original blessing that has caused pain to its recipient (perhaps because of abuse or other trials that have come to the blessing's recipient). In such a circumstance, a person may speak to their bishop and stake president about the possibility of receiving a second patriarchal blessing. While such scenarios are rare, where necessary, priesthood leaders can authorize a second blessing.

Notes

1. See John L. Lund, *Understanding Your Patriarchal Blessing* (Orem, UT: Noble Publishing, 1980), 68.
2. See Joseph F. Smith, "The Significance of Patriarchal Blessings," in *Conference Report*, October 1944, 112.
3. Eldred G. Smith, "What Is a Patriarchal Blessing?" *The Instructor* 97, no. 2 (February 1962): 43.
4. Gayla Wise, *The Power of Your Patriarchal Blessing* (Provo, UT: Spring Creek, 2007), 20.

—14—

What Do Patriarchal Blessings Have to Do with Christ—The Focus of All We Do in the Church?

Nephi wrote, "Behold . . . *all things* which have been given of God from the beginning of the world, unto man, are the typifying of him" (2 Nephi 11:4; emphasis added). Nephi's brother Jacob recorded, "Behold, I say unto you that none of the prophets have written, nor prophesied, save they have spoken concerning this Christ" (Jacob 7:11). In the book of Moses, the Lord Himself stated, "And behold, all things have their likeness, and all things are created and made to bear record of me" (Moses 6:63). Clearly, *all things* created by God were designed to teach about and testify of His Only Begotten Son.

So how does this truth apply to you and your patriarchal blessing? Well, there are a number of ways in which your blessing is designed to point you toward Christ. What follows is but a sampling.

First of all, your patriarchal blessing is filled with the inspired instructions you will need in order to become like Jesus, which is not only the ultimate goal of mortality but also the only way you or I can return to God to dwell with Him for eternity.

In addition, your patriarchal blessing is evidence of Heavenly Father's and Jesus's love for you. God evidences that love by offering you tremendous and sacred blessings not available to much of the world. Thus, these promises the Father (through Christ) has made to you should constantly point your mind (and your life) toward God and His Only Begotten Son.

Your blessing is also proof that, as a Christian, you have a right (if you remain worthy) to have His power active in your life. That power will protect you, but it will also advance you in the causes you undertake in life. It will allow you to succeed in both your secular and your sacred pursuits. Moreover, it will be the means by which you will have influence in the world.

Your patriarchal blessing shows that the Father has called you to be Christ's face, voice, and hands in the lives of your brothers and sisters—whom He sees as His spiritual sons and daughters. Jesus can't be everywhere, but, through His faithful followers, He can bless and touch each of God's children. Therefore, your patriarchal blessing is a calling to act as one of His covenant sons and daughters. It is a call to bless those whom God will place in your path.

Finally, just as the Father sent His Only Begotten Son to the earth with a sacred and foreordained mission, your patriarchal blessing proves that you too sustained the Father's plan and Christ's role in that plan in the Grand Council in Heaven and, thus, were foreordained to a sacred mortal mission that is an extension of Jesus's mission. If you keep your covenants and live faithful to your patriarchal blessing, you will fulfill the mission you were foreordained to.

In so many ways, your patriarchal blessing points you to Christ!

What Is a Patriarch?

"I have great confidence in the patriarchs and in their blessings. . . . The promises which he makes under his special authority and calling will be fulfilled."

President Spencer W. Kimball

"The Foundations of Righteousness,"
Ensign, November 1977.

—15—

What Is a Patriarch?

As we've already noted, the word PATRIARCH is Latin, and means "chief father."[1] Thus, the terms "father" and "patriarch" are synonyms; they mean basically the same thing.

There are many kinds of patriarchs. Heavenly Father is a patriarch over the entire human race. Your dad is a patriarch over your immediate family. The prophetic leaders of the Old Testament were typically called patriarchs because they watched over the Church, much like bishops, whom we refer to as the "fathers" of the ward.[2] Finally, patriarch is an office in the Melchizedek Priesthood.[3] The first of these four patriarchs, God the Father, is the source of all revelation. The other three have the ability to be the recipients of His revelation.

Speaking of stake patriarchs, the First Presidency has stated that they "should be men who have developed within them the spirit of the patriarchs."[4] What is the "spirit of the patriarchs"? It is the gift of prophecy (see D&C 46:22; Moroni 10:13; 1 Corinthians 12:10, 14:1). According to President Boyd K. Packer (1924–2015), former president of the Quorum of the Twelve Apostles, "A patriarch has prophetic insight."[5] President John Taylor (1808–1887), third President of the Church, taught, "The Patriarchs have the gift of being prophets, seers and revelators, to . . . portray unto the faithful their future lives."[6] Quite literally, a patriarch is a prophet—not for the whole Church but for those in the stake who have qualified themselves to receive a personal revelation from God through one of His authorized servants. President Spencer W. Kimball (1895–1985), twelfth President of the Church, said to stake patriarchs, "In a real sense, your voice is to give utterance to the message of the

Lord which he has in store for the individuals who come to you."[7] President Kimball added, "The patriarch is a prophet entitled to the revelations of the Lord to each individual on whose heads he places his hands."[8]

The calling and office of stake patriarch is unique in that it is a priesthood office—but it is a calling of blessing, not of administration or counseling. For example, the office of bishop has, as part of its duties, administrative responsibilities. The ordained bishop blesses, but he also counsels the members and administers the sacred funds of the Church as he runs the ward. A stake patriarch, on the other hand, is ordained to his priesthood office but doesn't counsel members, nor does he have any administrative duties. His calling, by virtue of his ordination, is simply to give blessings and nothing else.

Because stake patriarchs are prophets who receive personal revelation for members of a stake, President Boyd K. Packer indicated, "The office of stake patriarch . . . is essential to the spiritual power of a stake."[9] If members of a stake do not seek out and then study and apply their patriarchal blessings, the stake will be less spiritual, and the members will have less direction in their lives. Thus, what the patriarch is called to provide has the potential to elevate the level of spirituality in a ward or stake—*if* the members will prayerfully read and apply the counsel found in their individual patriarchal blessings.

The Prophet Joseph Smith taught, "An Evangelist is a Patriarch, even the oldest man of the blood of Joseph or of the seed of Abraham. Wherever the Church of Christ is established in the earth, there should be a Patriarch for the benefit of the posterity of the Saints, as it was with Jacob in giving his patriarchal blessing unto his sons."[10] For Latter-day Saints, the terms *evangelist* and *patriarch* are synonymous. They are used interchangeably in Mormonism. The Greek word translated *evangelist* (in Acts 21:8; 2 Timothy 4:5) means literally "a bringer of good tidings" or "a proclaimer of good news."[11] The verb of this same Greek root is typically translated (in the New Testament) "bring"—as in to "bring glad tidings" (Romans 10:15). For this reason, many Christian churches use the term *evangelist* to refer to someone who is a missionary—a proclaimer of the good news of the gospel.[12] However, a stake patriarch is certainly "a bringer of good tidings" or "a proclaimer of good news." Indeed, whereas some Christian missionaries proclaim a message of condemnation and pending doom, the patriarch's message is almost exclusively one of "good news" and, thus, the title *evangelist* seems appropriately applied to him. His calling and office in the priesthood are entirely about "bringing good tidings" to those who seek a blessing at his hands.

Notes

1. *Patriarchal Blessings* (Salt Lake City, UT: The Church of Jesus Christ of Latter-day Saints, 1979), 2.
2. John A. Widtsoe, *Priesthood and Church Government* (Salt Lake City, UT: Deseret Book, 1961), 125.
3. Boyd K. Packer, "The Stake Patriarch," *Ensign*, November 2002, 42.
4. James R. Clark, *Messages of the First Presidency*, vol. 4 (Salt Lake City, UT: Bookcraft, 1970), 58.
5. Packer, "The Stake Patriarch," 42.
6. John Taylor, in Conference Report, April 1902, 44.
7. Spencer W. Kimball, *The Teachings of Spencer W. Kimball*, Edward L. Kimball, comp. (Salt Lake City, UT: Bookcraft, 1998), 505.
8. Kimball, *The Teachings of Spencer W. Kimball*, 504.
9. Packer, "The Stake Patriarch," 45.
10. Joseph Smith, *Teachings of the Prophet Joseph Smith*, Joseph Fielding Smith, comp. (Salt Lake City, UT: Deseret Book, 1976), 151.
11. See Gerhard Kittle, ed., *Theological Dictionary of the New Testament*, Geoffrey W. Bromily, trans., 10 vols. (Grand Rapids, MI: Eerdmans, 1983), 2:707.
12. See Bruce R. McConkie, *Mormon Doctrine*, 2nd ed. (Salt Lake City, UT: Bookcraft, 1979), 241.

–16–

Since Patriarch Is an Office in the Melchizedek Priesthood, Is There a General Church Patriarch That Presides Over the Stake Patriarchs?

THE SHORT ANSWER TO THIS QUESTION IS *NO*. FOR MANY DECADES, the Church had a position known as Patriarch *to* the Church. The man who held this office was a General Authority, and he was an ordained patriarch. However, he was not a patriarch *over* the Church. He did not preside over a quorum of patriarchs. Indeed, patriarchs really have no quorum. On Sundays, they attend priesthood meetings with the High Priests.

The Patriarch to the Church was simply a patriarch who had no boundaries as it relates to whom he could bless. Whereas a stake patriarch can only give blessings to those who lived in the boundaries of his stake—or to his direct line descendants—the Patriarch to the Church "had overall jurisdiction and could give patriarchal blessings to any properly recommended member regardless of location."[1] When the Church was smaller and many members lived in missions instead of stakes, they didn't have access to a patriarch. Therefore, the Patriarch to the Church would provide their patriarchal blessings—in some cases, by traveling to where these members lived and, in other cases, by giving them blessings when they came to Salt Lake City.[2] However, today, with the growth of the Church, most members live in stakes or near enough to a stake that they can receive their patriarchal blessing at the hands of an ordained stake patriarch (who speaks their own language). Thus, the office of Patriarch to the Church was discontinued in October of 1979.

In the spirit of that which is declared in Doctrine and Covenants 107:40, the office of Patriarch to the Church was a hereditary office that passed through the lineal descendants of Joseph Smith Sr., who was the first ordained Patriarch to the Church in this final dispensation. For this reason, in Doctrine and Covenants 23:3, the Lord says to Hyrum Smith (Joseph Smith Sr.'s eldest son), "Thy duty is unto the church forever, and this because of thy family." In other words, Hyrum would have a duty to the Church (as patriarch) until he died, because he was born into the line of patriarchs to the Church, his father being the first, and he being the second. The heredity line of patriarchs to the Church, in this dispensation, is as follows:

- **Joseph Smith Sr.** (1771–1840)—who was the father of Joseph Smith, Jr., and who served as Patriarch to the Church from 1833 until 1840.
- **Hyrum Smith** (1800–1844)—who was the brother of Joseph Smith, Jr., and who served as Patriarch to the Church from 1841 until 1844.
- **William Smith** (1811–1893)—who was Joseph Jr.'s and Hyrum's brother, served as patriarch from May 24, 1845, until October 19, 1845. Because William insisted that he was patriarch *over* the Church—rather than *to* the church—he was excommunicated from the Church for his unwillingness to accept his subservient position to the Twelve.
- **John Smith** (1781–1854)—who was the brother of Joseph Smith Sr., and who served as Patriarch to the Church from 1847 until 1854.[3]
- **John Smith** (1832–1911)—who was Hyrum's eldest son, and who served as Patriarch to the Church from 1855 until 1911.
- **Hyrum Gibbs Smith** (1879–1932)—who was the great-grandson of Hyrum Smith, and who served as Patriarch to the Church from 1912 until 1932.
- **Joseph F. Smith II** (1899–1964)—who was the grandson of President Joseph F. Smith, served as Patriarch to the Church from 1942 until 1946.[4]
- **Eldred G. Smith** (1907–2013)—who was son of Hyrum Gibbs Smith, served as Patriarch to the Church from 1947 until 1979, when the office of Patriarch to the Church was discontinued, and Elder Smith was designated as patriarch emeritus.[5]

Each of the men serving in this office during its 146-year history was a descendant of Asael Smith, the father of Joseph Smith Sr. (the first Patriarch to the Church).

Notes

1. Gayla Wise, *The Power of Your Patriarchal Blessing* (Provo, UT: Spring Creek, 2007), 33.
2. See John L. Lund, *Understanding Your Patriarchal Blessing* (Orem, UT: Noble Publishing, 1980), 59.
3. Uncle John Smith, as he was known, was sustained as the Patriarch to the Church on December 6, 1847. However, he was not actually ordained to the office until January 1, 1849. See Irene M. Bates and E. Gary Smith, *Lost Legacy: The Mormon Office of Presiding Patriarch* (Urbana & Chicago, IL: University of Illinois Press, 2003), 107–108.
4. Between Hyrum G. Smith and Joseph F. Smith II, there was a space of ten years when there was no functioning Patriarch to the Church. During that time, Apostle George F. Richards functioned as "acting patriarch" until a Patriarch to the Church could be sustained and ordained. See Bates and Smith, *Lost Legacy*, 187.
5. See Lund, *Understanding Your Patriarchal Blessing*, 60–61.

—17—

Who Can Give a Patriarchal Blessing?

THE ANSWER TO THIS QUESTION IS TO BE FOUND IN WHAT ONE means by the word *patriarch*. As has already been pointed out, there are different kinds of patriarchs in the Church. This book has largely focused on the stake patriarch, who is certainly authorized to give patriarchal blessings to his lineal descendants and also to members of his stake. However, as we have noted already, prophets are also called *patriarchs*—though they do not traditionally give patriarchal blessings, even to their direct descendants. (This they leave to the stake patriarchs of the Church.) Your father, grandfather, great-grandfather, etc., if they are baptized members of the Church—and holders of the Melchizedek Priesthood—are "natural patriarchs" to their family and have the right to bestow what would appropriately be called a "patriarchal" or "father's blessing" upon *any* in their family who needs one. However, their service to their family is different from that of the stake patriarch. In an article he wrote in the *New Era*, Elder James E. Faust (1920–2007), then a member of the Quorum of the Twelve Apostles, cited a policy statement issued by the First Presidency of the Church regarding fathers—as natural patriarchs—giving blessings to their children.

> Certainly we should give new and additional emphasis to the role of the father in giving blessings to children in the family. We think we should generally leave to the ordained patriarchs in the stakes the responsibility of declaring lineage in connection with an official patriarchal blessing, but still we could leave unlocked the door so that any father who felt inspired to pronounce the lineage in connection with a father's blessing he was giving to his children should not be prevented from doing so.[1]

The point of the First Presidency letter, as cited by Elder Faust, is that fathers need to more fully embrace their role as patriarch for their posterity. They should give blessings frequently, and they should live in such a way that they can be inspired in their leadership of, and counsel to, their children and grandchildren. In the words of John A. Widtsoe (1872–1952), a member of the Quorum of the Twelve Apostles, "Every father, having children born to him under the covenant, is to them as a patriarch, and he has the right to bless his posterity in the authority of the Priesthood which he holds."[2]

That being said, it is the right and duty of a stake patriarch to give a singular (one-time) blessing that declares the recipient's lineage. The natural patriarch—or father—on the other hand, has the right and duty to *frequently* bless his children and grandchildren, but he has no "duty" to declare the lineage of the child being blessed. Whereas a blessing from a stake patriarch seeks to reveal things about the recipient's entire life, a blessing from one's father (or natural patriarch) will typically focus on the present or the near future of the recipient.[3]

One official Church publication on patriarchal blessings declared, "An ordained patriarch is an authorized substitute for all those whose fathers are either not in the Church or are unfit or unwilling to give blessings."[4] Substantiating this claim, President John Taylor (1808–1887), third President of the Church, wrote an editorial in the *Times & Seasons*—an early Mormon periodical. In that editorial, President Taylor noted the following:

> A Patriarch to the church is appointed to bless those who are orphans, or have no father in the church to bless them. . . .
>
> The above is the true doctrine of the church in regard to this matter, and we speak of it for the information of the brethren at large, lest those who may have received their patriarchal blessings . . . from their fathers, might be tempted to think they were of no avail. . . .
>
> Adam was the natural father of his posterity, who were his family and over whom he presided as patriarch. . . . Both Abraham and Jacob stood in the same relationship to their families. But not so with Father Joseph Smith, Hyrum Smith, or William Smith. They were not the natural fathers of the church, and could not stand in the same capacity as Adam, Abraham, or Jacob; but inasmuch as there had been none

to bless for generations past, according to the ancient order, they were ordained and set apart for the purpose of conferring patriarchal blessings, to hold the keys of this priesthood, and unlock the door, that had long been closed upon the human family: that blessings might again be conferred according to the ancient order, and those who were orphans, or had no father to bless them, might receive it through a patriarch who should act as proxy for their father, and that fathers might again be enabled to act as patriarchs to their families, and bless their children.[5]

President Taylor's point was that the reason we have stake patriarchs is that there are many members of the Church who do not have a father or grandfather who is an active member and who could pronounce upon them a patriarchal blessing. Thus, out of concern for those members, God revealed the office of stake patriarch—that all might receive a blessing from the Lord.[6] Anciently, it was the father's responsibility to bless his children.[7] Today, because so many do not have a father who can do so, this responsibility has largely fallen to the stake patriarchs. However, Elder Bruce R. McConkie (1915–1985) of the Quorum of the Twelve Apostles, suggested that during the Millennium, "Each person will receive his patriarchal blessing, we suppose from the natural patriarch who presides in his family, as it was in Adamic days and as it was when Jacob blessed his sons."[8]

Notes

1. James E. Faust, "Patriarchal Blessings," *New Era,* November 1982, 6–7. See also *Patriarchal Blessings* (Salt Lake City, UT: The Church of Jesus Christ of Latter-day Saints, 1979), 2.
2. John A. Widtsoe, *Evidences and Reconciliations,* 3rd ed. (Salt Lake City: Bookcraft, 1943), 72.
3. See Gayla Wise, *The Power of Your Patriarchal Blessing* (Provo, UT: Spring Creek, 2007), 22.
4. *Patriarchal Blessings,* 2.
5. John Taylor, "Patriarchal," Editorial in *Times and Seasons,* 6 vols. (Independence, MO: Independence Press, 1986), 6:921–922.
6. For this reason, when Joseph Smith Sr. gave patriarchal blessings, he would often refer to them as "father's blessings" to the "orphans" of the Church who

did not have a natural father who could give them their patriarchal blessing. See Gary Shepherd and Gordon Shepherd, *Binding Earth and Heaven: Patriarchal Blessings in the Prophetic Development of Early Mormonism* (University Park, PA: Pennsylvania State University Press, 2012), 53–54.

7. For sources that discuss a father's role, responsibility, and rights as a natural patriarch to his posterity, see John Taylor, *Gospel Kingdom*, G. Homer Durham, ed. (Salt Lake City, UT: Bookcraft, 1998), 146; Bruce R. McConkie, *Mormon Doctrine*, 2nd ed. (Salt Lake City, UT: Bookcraft, 1979), 560, 558; Taylor, "Patriarchal," Editorial in *Times and Seasons*, 6:921–922; Lesson 24, "Patriarchal Blessings," in *On Earth and in Heaven: A Course of Study of the Melchizedek Priesthood of The Church of Jesus Christ of Latter-day Saints* (Salt Lake City, UT: The First Presidency, 1967), 183–185; *General Handbook of Instructions*, no. 21 (1976), 50; Joseph Fielding Smith Jr., *Doctrines of Salvation*, 3 vols. (Salt Lake City, UT: Bookcraft, 1998), 3:172; John A. Widtsoe, *Evidences and Reconciliations*, 3 vols. (Salt Lake City, UT: Bookcraft, 1943), 1:72–73; First Presidency Statement, cited in Faust, "Patriarchal Blessings," 6–7; Bruce R. McConkie, *Millennial Messiah* (Salt Lake City, UT: Deseret Book, 1982), 673; Ed J. Pinegar and Richard J. Allen, *Your Patriarchal Blessing* (American Fork, UT: Covenant Communications, 2005), 86; Grant Von Harrison, *Fathers As Patriarchs* (Sandy, UT: Sounds of Zion, 1990), 4; Gayla Wise, *The Power of Your Patriarchal Blessing* (Provo, UT: Spring Creek, 2007), 34, 38.

8. McConkie, *Millennial Messiah*, 673.

—18—

How Is a Patriarch Called?

THE QUORUM OF THE TWELVE APOSTLES HAS THE DIVINELY appointed responsibility for calling patriarchs. In Doctrine and Covenants 107:39 we read, "It is the duty of the Twelve . . . to ordain [patriarchs], as they shall be designated unto them by revelation." In the early days of the Church, patriarchs were usually selected and ordained to their office by a member of the Quorum of the Twelve—or, occasionally, by a member of the First Presidency. However, as the Church has grown, it is no longer tenable for an apostle to travel to every stake in order to ordain a new patriarch when one is needed. Consequently, today, stake presidents fast and pray about whom they should recommend (or "nominate") to the Quorum of the Twelve to be ordained to the office of patriarch. The Twelve Apostles prayerfully consider the name and, if approved, authorize the stake president to ordain the man to the office of patriarch.[1] Like any other ordination in the Church, the stake patriarch is ordained by the laying on of hands. The only person authorized to ordain a patriarch (other than a member of the First Presidency or Quorum of the Twelve) is a stake president; and he does so, acting under the keys of the President of the Church. (Even another ordained patriarch is not permitted to ordain someone to that office in the Melchizedek Priesthood.)

President Thomas S. Monson (1927–2018), sixteenth President of the Church, shared the following about the inspiration behind the calling of stake patriarchs:

> Many years back I had been assigned to name a patriarch for a stake in Logan, Utah. I found such a man, wrote his name on a slip of paper, and placed the note inside my scriptures. My further review revealed

that another worthy patriarch had moved to this same area, making unnecessary the naming of a new patriarch. None was named.

Nine years later I was again assigned a stake conference in Logan. Once more a patriarch was needed for the stake I was to visit. I had been using a new set of scriptures for several years and had them in my briefcase. However, as I prepared to leave my home for the drive to Logan, I took from the bookcase shelf an older set of scriptures, leaving the new ones at home. During the conference I began my search for a patriarch: a worthy man, a blameless servant of God, one filled with faith, characterized by kindness. Pondering these requirements, I opened my scriptures and there discovered the slip of paper placed there long years before. I read the name written on the paper: Cecil B. Kenner. I asked the stake presidency if by chance Brother Kenner lived in this particular stake. I found he did. Cecil B. Kenner was that day ordained a patriarch.[2]

As is illustrated by this story, the Lord loves His members too much to allow the wrong man to be called as stake patriarch. He knows whom He wants as His patriarchs, and He knows how to inspire leaders to call the right man.

Notes

1. Boyd K. Packer, "The Stake Patriarch," *Ensign*, November 2002, 42–43.
2. Thomas S. Monson, "Your Patriarchal Blessing: A Liahona of Light," *Ensign*, November 1986, 65–66.

—19—

How Does a Patriarch Know What to Say in the Blessings He Pronounces?

ALL PATRIARCHAL BLESSINGS COME FROM GOD. THEY ARE REVELA-tions from the Father, and the patriarch is the revelator whom the Quorum of the Twelve Apostles has assigned to receive that rev-elation. Consequently, a patriarch must be a spiritual man who is seasoned in the gospel, who knows the doctrine, and who lives a life that is beyond reproach. He is a man who, over years of faithful service in priesthood callings, has learned how to receive revelation and has developed in his personal life the gift for recog-nizing the whisperings of the Holy Ghost. He is wise, dignified, and mature. Because he has been ordained to the office of patriarch (in the Melchizedek Priesthood), he has a right—by virtue of his priest-hood office—to receive revelation on behalf of others, so long as he lives his life in such a way so as to be receptive to God's Holy Spirit.

You should know that, in the days prior to giving you your blessing, the patriarch will pray specifically for you and about you dozens of times—seeking to see you as Heavenly Father sees you and to know you in ways he only could by revelation. Some patri-archs fast before they give blessings. Your patriarch will study his scriptures intently and be very cautious about what he watches or listens to in order to have the Spirit fully with him. He will be making significant sacrifices in his own life in order to be ready to bless you. These sacrifices will enable him to hear the voice of the Lord through God's Holy Spirit. These sacrifices will enable him to receive revelation about you *even before* he places his hands upon your head.

President Harold B. Lee (1899–1973), eleventh President of the Church, shared an experience he had when he ordained a man to be a stake patriarch:

> I was sent back years ago to New York to select a patriarch. We decided upon a certain man and went to his home. He had been out with his sons on the welfare farm pitching manure all day and was tired and weary. After he had changed his clothes and came in, I made him more weary when I told him what it was I had come for—that he was to be called as the patriarch to that stake.
>
> The next morning in conference he bore a remarkable testimony. Then afterwards we went to the Manhattan Ward, where I was to ordain him. The office is down in the basement where there is no natural light [because there was no window].
>
> This is the story as told by the stake president's wife: "As you walked over to put your hands on DeWitt Paul's head, I thought to myself, He is a man with whom we socialize. We have gone on trips with him, to dances, and he has been in our social group. Now part of his responsibility is to declare the lineage from which each one has come in these blessings. He hasn't been a student of ancient languages—how is he going to know?
>
> "With these thoughts in my mind, you walked over and put your hands on his head, and a light came from behind you and went right through you and into him. And I thought to myself, Isn't that a strange coincidence that the sunlight has come in just at that moment. And then I realized that there was no sunlight. I was witnessing the answer to my question. That light came from somewhere beyond Brother Lee and went through Brother Lee into this patriarch. Then I knew where he was going to get that information—by the revelations of Almighty God."[1]

Of this experience, President Boyd K. Packer (1924–2015), President of the Quorum of the Twelve Apostles said, "And so it must be. Whenever a patriarch is ordained or pronounces a blessing, that same light, though it may be unseen, is present. It empowers a patriarch to declare lineage and to give a prophetic blessing, notwithstanding that he himself may be a man of very ordinary capacity."[2] As I have noted, God is the one giving the blessing; not the stake patriarch. Thus, so long as the patriarch and the one receiving the blessing are worthy and prepared, God will pour out the light of revelation, inspiring the patriarch to say just what needs to be said. One stake patriarch shared his experience of giving a patriarchal blessing:

> I began to repeat the introductory sentence. . . . While I was doing this, although my eyes were closed, I felt that I was looking at a large placard on which was printed part of the blessing. I would read it and new words would appear. This happened a number of times. When no more words appeared I closed with an appropriate sentence.[3]

Of course, patriarchs all receive revelation in their own way. Some may see the words, as this patriarch did, and some may hear them. Others may just have impressions and feelings as to what they should say. Regardless of which of these is the case for your stake patriarch, the point is that God inspires them—because they are good and holy men and because God loves you so much that He will not leave the content of your blessing to chance. If the patriarch makes promises under the inspiration of the Holy Spirit—and by his ordained authority—you can rest assured, those promises *will* come to pass. President Thomas S. Monson (1927–2018) shared a story that illustrates this truth:

> Many years ago, a humble and faithful patriarch, Brother Percy K. Fetzer, was called to give patriarchal blessings to Church members living behind the Iron Curtain.
>
> Brother Fetzer went into the land of Poland in those dark days. The borders were sealed, and no citizens were permitted to leave. Brother Fetzer met with German Saints who had been trapped there when the borders were redefined following World War II and the land where they were living became part of Poland.
>
> Our leader among all of those German Saints was Brother Eric P. Konietz, who lived there with his wife and children. Brother Fetzer gave Brother and Sister Konietz and the older children patriarchal blessings.
>
> When Brother Fetzer returned to the United States, he called and asked if he could come visit with me. As he sat in my office, he began to weep. He said, "Brother Monson, as I laid my hands upon the heads of the members of the Konietz family, I made promises which cannot be fulfilled. I promised Brother and Sister Konietz that they would be able to return to their native Germany, that they would not be held captive by the arbitrary decisions of conquering countries and that they would be sealed together as a family in the house of the Lord. I promised their son that he would fill a mission, and I promised their daughter

that she would be married in the holy temple of God. You and I know that because of the closed borders, they will not be able to receive the fulfillment of those blessings. What have I done?"

I said, "Brother Fetzer, I know you well enough to know that you have done just what our Heavenly Father wanted you to do." The two of us knelt down beside my desk and poured out our hearts to our Heavenly Father, indicating that promises had been given to a devoted family pertaining to the temple of God and other blessings now denied to them. Only He could bring forth the miracle we needed.

The miracle occurred. A pact was signed between the leaders of the Polish government and the leaders of the Federal Republic of Germany, permitting German nationals who had been trapped in that area to move to West Germany. Brother and Sister Konietz and their children moved to West Germany, and Brother Konietz became the bishop of the ward in which they resided.

The entire Konietz family went to the holy temple in Switzerland. And who was the temple president who greeted them in a white suit with open arms? None other than Percy Fetzer—the patriarch who gave them the promise. Now, in his capacity as president of the Bern Switzerland Temple, he welcomed them to the house of the Lord, to the fulfillment of that promise, and sealed the husband and wife together and the children to their parents.

The young daughter eventually married in the house of the Lord. The young son received his call and fulfilled a full-time mission.[4]

God inspires his stake patriarchs. Even they, at times, may be surprised by the miraculous promises He makes to His children; but God will always bring to pass the promises made through His appointed servants.

Regarding the content of your blessing, one stake patriarch explained, "Many [patriarchal blessings] are accompanied by the feeling that we have heard [their contents] before. . . . You may have similar feelings when you receive your blessing. [This familiar feeling] is often a recall of your premortal knowledge weaved within the vocabulary of the patriarch."[5] In other words, if what the patriarch says to you feels strangely familiar, it may be because your spirit recognizes these promises from when you were in the premortal existence—when those very same promises were made to you by your Father in Heaven.

As it relates to how patriarchs know how to do what they have been called by God to do, perhaps one other point is worth making. In addition to their ordination, stake patriarchs are given training to assist them in their assignment. Of course, they are not novices. Their years of Church service helps to prepare them for their calling as patriarch. There is also a handbook for stake patriarchs, which gives them guidance and counsel on what it means to be a patriarch and on how to give inspired blessings. Furthermore, in 2005, the Church held a worldwide leadership training meeting, in which they taught patriarchs about their calling. (The transcript from this training meeting is given to all newly called stake patriarchs.) Stake presidents are also assigned to periodically read some of the blessings given by the patriarch and to offer general suggestions, advice, and encouragement. Most stake patriarchs meet with their stake president once a year to discuss their calling and to receive counsel or guidance from him. (Twice a year the stake president should review some of the blessings the patriarch has given.) It shouldn't be forgotten that a patriarch has his own patriarchal blessing, which can help him in understanding what the blessings he gives should be. One source pointed out, "A patriarch can go to a reading room in Salt Lake City and read blessings in a collection from the last seventy years."[6] For a new stake patriarch, doing this might help him to get a sense of his calling and of the nature of patriarchal blessings.

Notes

1. Harold B. Lee, *The Teachings of Harold B. Lee*, Clyde J. Williams, comp. (Salt Lake City, UT: Bookcraft, 1998), 488–89.
2. Boyd K. Packer, "The Stake Patriarch," *Ensign*, November 2002, 45.
3. Urvin Gee, cited in Gayla Wise, *The Power of Your Patriarchal Blessing* (Provo, UT: Spring Creek, 2007), 78.
4. Thomas S. Monson, "Blessings of the Temple," *Ensign*, November 2010, 16–17.
5. Garry H. Boyle, *A Loving Letter from God: Your Patriarchal Blessing* (Springville, UT: Cedar Fort, 2015), 70.
6. Wise, *The Power of Your Patriarchal Blessing*, 87.

—20—

Would a Different Patriarch Give Me the Exact Same Blessing?

NO TWO PATRIARCHS WOULD GIVE, WORD FOR WORD, THE SAME blessing.[1] However, there is a reason for that. Elder John A. Widtsoe (1872–1952) of the Quorum of the Twelve Apostles explained, "Since patriarchs are but men, . . . their manner of speech and thinking is reflected in their blessings. Different men express the same idea in different words. The Lord does not dictate blessings to them word for word. . . . Nevertheless, if the patriarch lives worthily, he is sustained by the power and authority of his calling, and will pronounce blessings intended for us."[2] In other words, regardless of how many patriarchs gave you your blessing, similar themes would likely be discussed in each. Yet it is important to know that God gives the patriarch the *truths* that should be spoken, but He often leaves it up to the patriarch to articulate those truths—to the best of his ability—in his own *language*. Consequently, were three different patriarchs to give you a patriarchal blessing, each might bless you with the gift of tongues. However, one might say something like, "You will have a gift for languages;" another might say, "You will be endowed with the gift to convey the truths of the gospel to people in a way that they will be able to clearly understand them;" and another might simply say, "You will have the gift of tongues." The blessing is the same, but the way a given patriarch will express that would surely vary from patriarch to patriarch. One author explained it this way:

> Blessings from two patriarchs might be comparable to the same scene painted by two different artists. There would be many differences in the

finished painting (as in word choices compared to brush strokes), but the two pictures would have the same content. If they were at different times, they might be affected by the season or changes in the landscape but still have the same elements in the picture.[3]

In addition, the age at which you receive your blessing would also influence what a patriarch would tell you. What a patriarch would bless you with at sixteen is not likely to be the same as what he would bless you with if you were receiving your blessing at sixty-six. For example, if the sixteen-year-old were receiving his blessing, there might be counsel regarding selecting a mate. However, if a sixty-six-year-old had been happily married for forty years—and was still married at the time he or she received a patriarchal blessing—there would be no counsel given about choosing a mate. Thus, the stage of life you are in influences the blessings the Lord chooses to reveal. That would be true if the same patriarch was blessing you at sixteen or sixty-six. The content would vary because your needs at that stage of life would be different.

Notes

1. Eldred G. Smith, "What Is a Patriarchal Blessing?" *The Instructor* 97, no. 2 (February 1962): 43.
2. John A. Widtsoe, *Evidences and Reconciliations*, vol. 1 (Salt Lake City, UT: Bookcraft, 1943), 76.
3. Garry H. Boyle, *A Loving Letter from God: Your Patriarchal Blessing* (Springville, UT: Cedar Fort, 2015), 158.

–21–

How Do You Refer to a Patriarch?

WHILE IT MAY FEEL QUITE NATURAL TO CALL THE PATRIARCH BY his title (i.e., "Patriarch Smith"), we are encouraged to instead call him "Brother so-and-so" rather than "Patriarch so-and-so."

When we had a general Church Patriarch—or Patriarch *to* the Church—he was referred to as "Elder Smith" because he was a General Authority. However, stake patriarchs are not general authorities, and they should simply be referred to as "Brother so-and-so."[1]

One source explained, "If you were ever called upon to introduce a stake patriarch to a friend or to a formal gathering of people you would not say, 'This is Patriarch so and so'; rather, you would say, 'I would like to introduce . . . Brother so and so who is the Patriarch in such and such a stake.'"[2]

Notes

1. See James E. Talmage, "The Honor and Dignity of the Priesthood," in *Messages of the First Presidency*, vol. 4 (Salt Lake City, UT: Bookcraft, 1970), 308.
2. John L. Lund, *Understanding Your Patriarchal Blessing* (Orem, UT: Noble Publishing, 1980), 57.

—22—

Why Does the Patriarch Sit on the Stand during Stake Conference?

THOUGH THE PATRIARCH'S OFFICE IS ONE OF BLESSING RATHER than one of administration or counseling, he sits on the stand during stake conference (or stake priesthood meetings) in order to remind the members of the stake of the sacred office which he holds. In addition, looking out over the congregation may help the patriarch to feel of the spirits of the members of the stake, for whom he has a responsibility to receive revelation (in the context of his calling).[1]

His presence on the rostrum is also as a reminder of the fact that a patriarchal blessing is available to all who qualify themselves to receive one. By his presence on the stand, it is hoped that those who have yet to receive their patriarchal blessing might be motivated to obtain it.

Seeing the patriarch on the stand may also remind those who have already received their blessing of the importance of regularly reading it. It may bring to their remembrance some of the significant blessings God has promised them if they are faithful to their covenants.

One stake patriarch I know suggested that having the patriarch sit on the stand during stake conference helps the youth know him and therefore may make them more comfortable going to him for a blessing.

Finally, his presence on the stand is a testament to everyone that revelation is foundational to the restored gospel, not simply on a general level, but also on a local level. Because we reverence the sacred and revelatory office which he holds and because of all his presence reminds us of, our patriarch sits on the stand during our stake conferences.

Note

1. See Garry H. Boyle, *A Loving Letter from God: Your Patriarchal Blessing* (Springville, UT: Cedar Fort, 2015), 148.

—23—

Can I Go to the Stake Patriarch to Get a Blessing Other than a Patriarchal Blessing?

SOME MIGHT ASSUME THAT THE STAKE PATRIARCH HAS A SPECIAL power that makes his blessings more spiritual or inspired than another priesthood holder—such as one's father or home teacher. While it is true that a stake patriarch holds the Melchizedek Priesthood and can certainly give blessings of healing, comfort, guidance, etc., nevertheless—other than when he acts in the office of patriarch (which he only does when giving patriarchal blessings)—his blessings are the same as any other worthy priesthood holder's, and he should not be called upon to give a blessing that a father, husband, or other Melchizedek Priesthood holder (within your line of authority) could give. In other words, if your father is an elder or high priest and is worthy, you should go to him (as your natural patriarch)—and not to the stake patriarch—if you are in need of a blessing for health, comfort, or guidance. If your father is unable, you should turn to another worthy family member, your home teachers, or your quorum president or bishop if you need such a blessing. While the patriarch has a special power given to him (by virtue of his priesthood office) to pronounce patriarchal blessings, for any other blessing, he has no more inspiration or power than any other holder of the Melchizedek Priesthood does.[1]

Note

1. See John L. Lund, *Understanding Your Patriarchal Blessing* (Orem, UT: Noble Publishing, 1980), 67–68.

Understanding Your Patriarchal Lineage

"Patriarchal blessings contemplate an inspired
declaration of the lineage of the recipient."

The First Presidency

First Presidency letter to stake
presidents, 28 June 1958.

—24—

What Are the Tribes of Israel, and from Which Tribe Are Most Members of the Church?

THE GREAT-GRANDSONS OF ABRAHAM, BORN TO JACOB, BECAME known as the twelve tribes of Israel. Each of these sons stood at the head of his tribe or family. Because of Joseph's unwavering faithfulness, he was given the birthright, which included a double portion of his father's inheritance. Joseph's two sons—Ephraim and Manasseh—were adopted by their grandfather and were given a place among the tribes of Israel. Thus, they took the place of Reuben and Simeon as possessors of the rights and blessings of the first and second born—which Reuben and Simeon had lost because of their lack of faithfulness.[1]

Technically, with Jacob's twelve sons (Reuben, Simeon, Levi, Judah, Dan, Naphtali, Gad, Asher, Issachar, Zebulun, Joseph, and Benjamin) and then Joseph's two boys (Ephraim and Manasseh) that Jacob adopted, you have fourteen groups or potential tribes. However, Joseph's birthright blessing—or double portion—went to his two sons instead of to him, which moves the number of tribes down to thirteen. Additionally, the tribe of Levi received no land inheritance because they were the tribe of Moses and Aaron and were to be scattered among all of the tribes, that they might provide priesthood ordinances for each of the other tribes. Thus, that brings the number of the tribes of Israel who received a land inheritance down to twelve.

The tribes of Israel are God's covenant people. To be "gathered in" means to join the Church, be baptized, receive the Holy Ghost—and the other ordinances and covenants of salvation—and then to live faithful to those. Whether you are literally of one of the tribes of

Israel or are adopted into a tribe, you become "of Israel" by joining God's Church (The Church of Jesus Christ of Latter-day Saints) and through making sacred covenants with Him. Receiving your patriarchal blessing allows you to formally know which of the tribes you belong to and through which you will receive your blessings. (When you receive your patriarchal blessing and your lineage is declared, you may be found to be from *any* of the twelve sons of Jacob, or from his grandsons, Ephraim and Manasseh.)

Under the leadership of Joshua, the tribes of Israel took possession of the land of Canaan. In 930 BC, the ten tribes (Asher, Dan, Ephraim, Gad, Issachar, Manasseh, Naphtali, Reuben, Simeon, and Zebulun)—often called "lost tribes of Israel"—formed the independent Kingdom of Israel in the north, and the two other tribes (Judah and Benjamin) set up the Kingdom of Judah in the south. After the Assyrians conquered the northern kingdom (in 721 BC), the ten tribes were gradually assimilated by other peoples and thus slowly lost their identity as organized tribes.

The scriptures frequently speak of the lost tribes as being in the "north" or as returning "from the north" (for examples, see Isaiah 43:6; Jeremiah 3:18, 16:15, 23:8, 31:8; Zechariah 2:6). However, in biblical Hebrew, there are two major words that are frequently translated "north": *tsawfone*', which literally means "dark," "hidden," or "gloomy";[2] and *semole*', which literally means "left hand" (or, by implication, non-covenant).[3] There is one additional Hebrew word which is occasionally rendered "north," *mezawreh*', which means "scatterer."[4] Consequently, the literal scriptural meaning of "north" is not geographic. Rather, it is a statement about the spiritual state of the one labeled as in the "north." When the "lost" tribes are said to "return" from the "north," the implied meaning is that they will come out of darkness and apostasy and enter into the covenant.[5] Although some in the Church assume that the "lost" tribes will literally return from some hidden land in the north, it should be remembered that numerous passages in the Old Testament, New Testament, and Doctrine and Covenants indicate that the "lost" tribes are scattered throughout the *entire earth* (see Deuteronomy 30:3; Amos 9:9; Zechariah 7:14; Luke 21:24; Jeremiah 30:3; Jacob 5:30; and D&C 45:24–25). Thus, the scriptural phrase "being in the north" most likely means that they are outside of the Church—wherever they are currently physically located. It traditionally means that they have "lost" or forgotten their spiritual identity. To be "lost" means you don't understand God's plan and your place in it. To be "found" or "gathered" means you have found and embraced the truth—and have entered into sacred covenants (such as that of baptism) and have received your patriarchal blessing.[6]

Based on patriarchal blessings given and the divinely revealed role of each of the tribes, we know that most members of the Church today are from the tribe of Ephraim.[7] Manasseh is the second most common lineage declared in the blessings of members of the Church today. There are also quite a few in the Church whose lineage is that of the tribe of Judah. While individuals from *every* tribe have been found, at this time in the history of the Church, most are going to be from the aforementioned three tribes, with Ephraim leading the way—as is his divine right.

Notes

1. See John L. Lund, *Understanding Your Patriarchal Blessing*, 33.
2. See Francis Brown, S. R. Driver, and Charles A. Briggs, eds., *A Hebrew and English Lexicon of the Old Testament* (Peabody, MA: Hendrickson Publishers, 1999), 860; Joel F. Drinkard, Jr., "North" in David Noel Freedman, ed., *The Anchor Bible Dictionary* (New York: Doubleday, 1992), 4:1135; James Strong, "Dictionary of the Hebrew Bible," in *The New Strong's Exhaustive Concordance of the Bible* (Nashville: Thomas Nelson Publishers, 1990), #6828.
3. Drinkard, "North" (1992), 4:1135; Allen C. Myers, *The Eerdmans Bible Dictionary* (Grand Rapids, MI: Eerdmans, 1987), 768. The right hand is the covenant hand.
4. See Job 37:9; Myers, *The Eerdmans Bible Dictionary*, 768.
5. See John L. McKenzie, *Dictionary of the Bible* (Milwaukee: The Bruce Publishing Company, 1965), S.v. "North," 620; J. F. McCurdy, "North," in James Hastings, ed., *Dictionary of the Bible* (New York: Charles Scribner's Sons, 1963), 701.
6. For a more extensive treatment of this concept, see Alonzo L. Gaskill, *The Lost Language of Symbolism: An Essential Guide for Recognizing and Interpreting Symbols of the Gospel* (Salt Lake City, UT: Deseret Book, 2003), 162–166.
7. Boyd K. Packer, "The Stake Patriarch," *Ensign*, November 2002, 44.

—25—

What Is the Purpose of Declaring One's Lineage in a Patriarchal Blessing?

PRESIDENT BOYD K. PACKER (1924–2015), FORMER PRESIDENT OF the Quorum of the Twelve Apostles, taught, "An essential part of a patriarchal blessing is the declaration of lineage. . . . This is very important."[1] Indeed, in the Church we place great emphasis on knowing one's lineage—and it is frequently said that one's lineage is a *vital* part of a patriarchal blessing. Some authors have suggested that it is the *most* important part of the blessing. But why? Why is it so important to know your lineage? What does it matter if you are a descendant of Israel or if you are from this tribe or that? There are several reasons why your lineage is important.

First of all, knowing that you are of the house of Israel helps you to realize that you were among the most valiant of God's spirit offspring in the premortal world. Elder Bruce R. McConkie (1915–1985) of the Quorum of the Twelve Apostles explained, "The whole house of Israel, known and segregated out from their fellows, was [in the premortal existence] inclined toward spiritual things."[2] Similarly, Elder Melvin J. Ballard (1873–1939), also a member of the Quorum of the Twelve Apostles, taught that covenant Israel is "a group of souls tested, tried, and proven before they were born into the world. . . . Through this lineage were to come the true and tried souls that had demonstrated their righteousness in the spirit world before they came here" to earth.[3] Consequently, the declaration of your lineage (in your patriarchal blessing) is also a declaration of your faithfulness in the premortal existence. It is a statement about your commitment to God and His plan of salvation before you were ever born into mortality. Robert L. Millet and Joseph Fielding McConkie explained, "The declaration of our lineage by patriarchs is as much a statement about who and what we *were* as it is about who we are now and what we may become."[4]

Second, knowing your lineage allows you to know that you have a right to certain blessings that not all of God's children will have access to during their mortal probation.[5] For example, Seth received from Adam the promise that "his posterity should be the chosen of the Lord, and that they should be preserved unto the end of the earth" (D&C 107:41–42). Abraham, who was a descendant of Seth, was similarly promised, "And I will bless them that bless thee, and curse him that curseth thee: and in thee shall all families of the earth be blessed" (Genesis 12:3; see also Genesis 22:18; Abraham 2:9–11). This blessing was renewed with Isaac (Genesis 26:3–4), Abraham's son, and then again with Jacob (Genesis 28:13–14, 35:11–12), Abraham's grandson—whose name would be changed by the Lord to "Israel" (he being the father of the tribes of Israel). At Sinai, God renewed these same covenants with the descendants of Abraham, Isaac, and Jacob—who had followed the prophet Moses (Exodus 19:1–8). Abraham was assured by the Lord that all of the blessings promised to him would be offered to *all* of his mortal posterity, provided they remained faithful (see D&C 132:29–50; Abraham 2:6–11). Eldred G. Smith (1907–2013), general Patriarch to the Church, taught, "When a person receives a patriarchal blessing, he is entitled to receive a pronouncement of the blessings of Israel, or a declaration of the tribe of Israel through which his blessings shall come. This is the right to the blessings of those recorded in the book of remembrance started in the days of Adam"—which blessings were renewed with *each* of the ancient patriarchs, and ultimately with *all* of Abraham's seed.[6] As one who was faithful in the pre-mortal world, you have a right to those blessings. By learning that you are of the house of Israel, you can know for certain that you are an heir to—that you have a divine right to—*all* of the blessings pronounced upon Abraham, Isaac, and Jacob. One source suggested, "Your patriarchal blessing is the Lord's sacred way of letting you know that you belong to His fold."[7] One stake patriarch explained, "The covenant God made with Abraham is renewed with you."[8] Similarly, Sister Julie B. Beck (b. 1954), former General President of the Relief Society, taught, "In your blessing, you are told about your ancestry in the house of Israel. That's your family line and your family line is sometimes called a tribe. All of the tribes go back to the great patriarch Abraham. Your lineage is important. It means that you are included in the promises given to Abraham that through him all the nations of the world would be blessed."[9] These blessings to Abraham and his descendants (which are known as the "Abrahamic Covenant") include, among other things, the following promises:

- You will be blessed with *innumerable posterity* (D&C 132:30; see also Genesis 12:7, 13:1–15:8, 17:4–8). While you may have many descendants here in mortality, ultimately, this promise means that in the celestial kingdom, when you have become like your heavenly parents, you too will have the power to preside over "worlds without number" (Moses 1:33–35), populated by your spirit children.[10]

- You will be blessed to receive the *promised land* (Abraham 2:6, 19; see also Genesis 12:2, 15:8). Traditionally, the "promised land" is understood not to be a physical location upon this telestial earth but, instead, as a symbol of the celestial kingdom.[11] In other words, God is promising you that, if you hold out faithful, you will be exalted.

- You will be *blessed above measure* (Abraham 2:9; Genesis 12:2). In this promise, God guarantees covenant Israel—all those who have been baptized and received their patriarchal blessing—that they will partake of God's most choice blessings. So great will be the blessings of those who enter into and keep sacred covenants that we will not be able to count them. In addition, once this life is through, you are promised, contingent upon your faithfulness, "all that [the] Father hath" (D&C 84:38).

- You are promised that *your name will be great among nations* (Abraham 2:9; Genesis 12:2–3). This blessing offers a unique and somewhat unexpected promise. Here, God guarantees you and me a form of status and acknowledgment—something we would not normally expect God to bestow upon us. Even in our day, when many reject God, still, there are people in *all nations* who acknowledge the existence of a divine being. Thankfully, many *still* hold their Creator in high regard, humbly acknowledging His blessings upon them each and every day. Ultimately, when you and I become as He is, we too will be "great among nations." When we are exalted and reside with our Heavenly Father for eternity—doing as He does and living as He lives—we too will receive the esteem of our creations. Until then, if we keep our covenants during this life—including our covenant to regularly attend the temple—we will be held in "great" esteem by those we redeem in the house of the Lord. Individuals from all nations will bow down to us in the eternities and will call us blessed because we provided for them the saving ordinances of the temple, which they could not do for themselves.

- You are promised that *you and your posterity will have the priesthood* (Abraham 2:9, 11). God created the worlds via His priesthood power. In the eternities, all that happens is based on priesthood power. You and I, whether male or female, are set apart for our callings and, in those settings apart, are given priesthood authority to act and serve as God would have us.[12] We have access to daily blessings because of the priesthood in our homes, ordinances at church and in the temple, and living prophets and apostles who hold all priesthood keys. The rest of the world does not have access to these great blessings, but God has freely given these things to you and me because we are descendants of Abraham—through one of the tribes of Israel. "As the seed of Abraham, we have a great responsibility regarding the salvation of mankind here upon the earth, for our commission is to carry the gospel message to the entire world."[13]

- You are promised that *all who receive the gospel will become your children* (Abraham 2:10). Thus, Paul spoke of Timothy—one of his converts—as "my own son in the faith" (1 Timothy 1:2; see also 2 Timothy 1:2, 2:1). The "doctrine of adoption" says that, when one accepts the gospel and enters into (and keeps) sacred covenants, one becomes a "son" or "daughter" of Christ. In other words, one is "adopted" into the "family of God." Presumably, when we become as the Father is, our spirit children too will be "adopted" back into our fold based on their willingness to accept and keep sacred covenants.

- You are promised that *those who bless you will be blessed; those who curse you will be cursed* (Abraham 2:11). Certainly, those who bless us in mortality *should be* blessed—particularly by us and out of our gratitude for their graciousness toward us. No doubt, God too will bless those who are kind to His covenant people. However, the promise that "those who curse us will be cursed" most likely will have its fulfillment in the next life. Thus, Nephi informs us, "the time surely must come that all they who fight against Zion shall be cut off" (1 Nephi 22:19).

All of these promises were made to Abraham and are available to you because you are a faithful member of the house of Israel.

Finally, knowing your lineage enables you to know which of the tribes you will receive your promised blessings through. For example, my mother's maiden name is Pappas and my father's surname is Gaskill. Thus, from the tribes (or families) of Pappas and Gaskill I get my heritage, culture, and blessings. In a similar way, by knowing which of the tribes of Israel you belong to, you learn of where your blessings come from and what specific blessings and responsibilities will be uniquely yours. One official Church publication on patriarchal blessings states:

> Each tribe received a blessing from Jacob as pronounced upon the head of the father of the tribe. These are contained in Genesis 49. Your patriarchal blessing is uniquely your own in addition to the one received by the head of your tribe. Receiving your lineage is probably the most important part of your blessing, for it gives you the right, based on your faithfulness, to the blessings of Abraham, Isaac, and Jacob.[14]

In other words, each of the tribes of Israel received a patriarchal blessing from Jacob (or Israel). Each of those ancient tribal patriarchal blessings make certain promises, assign certain responsibilities, or give certain warnings to a specific tribe.[15] Thus, by knowing your tribe, you are able to go to the scriptures and read about the patriarchal blessing originally pronounced upon all those of your same lineage. This is akin to a second patriarchal blessing for you. Or, as one author explained it, "you have two missions to fulfill in this life. One mission is a tribal or group mission; your other mission is your personal or individual mission."[16] As a member of the house of Israel, and as a descendant (literally or by adoption) of one of the tribes, you are "entitled to participate in these same blessings."[17] "You are tied to their missions and, through them, to Abraham and God's covenants."[18] By studying passages, like Genesis 49, you can learn about blessings promised to those of your tribe or warnings given to all those with the same lineage as you. To know such things will help keep you from sin, will assist you in learning your divine duties, and will help you to fulfill the specific callings God has for you in this life.

These many remarkable promised blessings are why the declaration of your lineage is so important. Through your declared lineage—and through your faithfulness—God promises you all these things, *and even more!*

Notes

1. Boyd K. Packer, "The Stake Patriarch," *Ensign*, November 2002, 44.
2. Bruce R. McConkie, *The Mortal Messiah*, 4 vols. (Salt Lake City, UT: Deseret Book, 1979–1981), 1:23.
3. Melvin J. Ballard, in *Crusader for Righteousness*, Melvin R. Ballard, comp. (Salt Lake City, UT: Bookcraft, 1966), 218–219.
4. Robert L. Millet and Joseph Fielding McConkie, *Our Destiny: The Call and Election of the House of Israel* (Salt Lake City, UT: Deseret Book, 1993), 18.
5. See Millet and McConkie, *Our Destiny*, 17.
6. Eldred G. Smith, "All May Share in Adam's Blessing," *Ensign*, June 1971.
7. Ed J. Pinegar and Richard J. Allen, *Your Patriarchal Blessing* (American Fork, UT: Covenant Communications, 2005), 4.
8. Garry H. Boyle, *A Loving Letter from God: Your Patriarchal Blessing* (Springville, UT: Cedar Fort, 2015), 36.
9. Julie B. Beck, "You Have a Noble Birthright," *Ensign*, May 2006, 106.
10. See Gayla Wise, *The Power of Your Patriarchal Blessing* (Provo, UT: Spring Creek, 2007), 27.
11. See Wise, *The Power of Your Patriarchal Blessing*, 27.
12. Dallin H. Oaks, "The Keys and Authority of the Priesthood," *Ensign*, May 2014, 49, 51.
13. Pinegar and Allen, *Your Patriarchal Blessing*, 11.
14. *Patriarchal Blessings* (Salt Lake City, UT: The Church of Jesus Christ of Latter-day Saints, 1979), 2.
15. Pinegar and Allen, *Your Patriarchal Blessing*, 15.
16. John L. Lund, *Understanding Your Patriarchal Blessing* (Orem, UT: Noble Publishing, 1980), 4, 29; Boyle, *A Loving Letter from God*, 41.
17. Pinegar and Allen, *Your Patriarchal Blessing*, 78.
18. Boyle, *A Loving Letter from God*, 137.

—26—

Is It Possible for Me to Be from a Different Lineage or Tribe than My Parents or Siblings?

YOUR PATRIARCHAL LINEAGE IS *NOT* DETERMINED PRIMARILY BY your race or nationality and, thus, it is not a statement about your genetics. In other words, when the patriarch declares what tribe of Israel you are from, he is not declaring your literal bloodline, as almost every human being is of mixed blood.[1] You and I almost certainly have the blood of *several* of the tribes of Israel coursing through our veins. Indeed, President Joseph Fielding Smith (1876–1972), tenth President of the Church, wrote, "It is true that we are [each] of mixed lineage. A man said to be of the lineage of Ephraim may also be a 'descendant of Reuben, Benjamin, or Simeon,' but the blood that predominates is the one that counts."[2] (See D&C 86:9.) Because the tribes of Israel were scattered throughout all the earth, the lineage or blood of Israel can be found among all races and nationalities. One stake patriarch explained:

> It was because of God's great love for all mankind that He made sure [that Abraham's] descendants through the tribes of Israel were scattered and brought to most parts of the world. That ensured that those blessings and yearnings for the gospel might be found in all the families of the earth, and that they might feel moved upon by the Spirit to desire the eternal blessings of the Abrahamic covenant.[3]

Because your lineage is a declaration of the line through which you will receive your blessings—and not solely a statement about what blood you have in your veins—it is entirely possible (though not necessarily extremely common) that a child can be of a different lineage than his or her parents or siblings. Again, most people are of mixed lineage.[4] Consequently, the declaration of your tribe is a statement about what line your blessings will come from. It is a statement about what blessings and responsibilities are yours. It may even be a statement about which bloodline is most dominant in you. However, it does not mean that you are somehow disconnected from other family members who have a different declared lineage. It simply implies that God has a slightly different work for you to do in building up His kingdom. Being of a different lineage than your parents or siblings "is not much different from a family that has blue-eyed, brown-eyed, and maybe hazel-eyed children."[5] You are still part of the family. You just have different traits and gifts.

Notes

1. Eldred G. Smith, "Patriarchal Blessings," address given at the Salt Lake Institute of Religion, January 17, 1964, 3.
2. Joseph Fielding Smith, *Answers to Gospel Questions*, 5 vols. (Salt Lake City, UT: Deseret Book, 1993), 5:167.
3. Garry H. Boyle, *A Loving Letter from God: Your Patriarchal Blessing* (Springville, UT: Cedar Fort, 2015), 116.
4. Boyd K. Packer, "The Stake Patriarch," *Ensign*, November 2002, 45.
5. Gayla Wise, *The Power of Your Patriarchal Blessing* (Provo, UT: Spring Creek, 2007), 17.

—27—

Does It Matter If I Am Literally of the Blood of Israel or Adopted into the House of Israel?

IN SOME PATRIARCHAL BLESSINGS, IT STATES THAT THE RECIPIENT is "a descendant" of this tribe or that. In others, the person being blessed is told that they are "adopted into" a given tribe. *True to the Faith* states, "It does not matter if your lineage in the house of Israel is through bloodlines or by adoption. As a member of the Church, you are counted as a descendant of Abraham and an heir to all the promises and blessings contained in the Abrahamic covenant."[1] All that matters is that you accept Christ and His gospel and then seek to comply with His covenants and commandments. If you do that, the blessings are the same, whether you are naturally of the blood of Israel, or adopted into the family of Abraham. The Prophet Joseph Smith taught:

> The Holy Ghost has no other effect than pure intelligence. It is more powerful in expanding the mind, enlightening the understanding, and storing the intellect with present knowledge, of a man who is of the literal seed of Abraham, than one that is a Gentile, though it may not have half as much visible effect upon the body; for as the Holy Ghost falls upon one of the literal seed of Abraham, it is calm and serene; and his whole soul and body are only exercised by the pure spirit of intelligence; while the effect of the Holy Ghost upon a Gentile, is to purge out the old blood, and make him actually of the seed of Abraham. That man that has none of the blood of Abraham (naturally) must have a new creation by the Holy Ghost. In such a case, there may be more of a powerful effect upon the body, and visible to the eye, than

73

upon an Israelite, while the Israelite at first might be far before the Gentile in pure intelligence.[2]

The Prophet Joseph was saying that, for those who are not literally "of the seed of Abraham," the Holy Ghost—once it comes upon them—will actually change their blood, making them literally a descendant of Abraham. Thus, if your blessing says you are "adopted" into the house of Israel—or if it states you are "entitled to the blessings of Abraham, Isaac, and Jacob" (rather than declaring you to be of a specific lineage)—this should not cause concern or disappointment. According to the prophet, once the Spirit comes upon you, you will have the blood of Israel coursing through your veins. President James E. Faust (1920–2007), Second Counselor in the First Presidency, taught, "No one need assume that he or she will be denied any blessing by reason of not being of the blood lineage of Israel. The Lord told Abraham, 'And I will bless them through thy name; for as many as receive this Gospel shall be called after thy name, and shall be accounted thy seed, and shall rise up and bless thee, as their father.' [Abraham 2:10]"[3] Thus, it makes absolutely no difference if you are "born of Israel" or are "entitled to the blessings" of Israel through "adoption." The blessings are the same. You are "accounted as the seed of Abraham" and have a right to all the promises made to him and his faithful posterity.

Notes

1. *True to the Faith: A Gospel Reference* (Salt Lake City, UT: The Church of Jesus Christ of Latter-day Saints, 2004), 112.
2. Joseph Smith, *Teachings of the Prophet Joseph Smith*, Joseph Fielding Smith, comp. (Salt Lake City, UT: Deseret Book, 1976), 149–150.
3. James E. Faust, "Priesthood Blessings," *Ensign*, November 1995, 83.

—28—

What If My Patriarch Forgets to Declare My Lineage When He Gives Me My Patriarchal Blessing?

WHILE IT IS RARE, BECAUSE THE INSPIRATION FROM HEAVEN CAN come upon the patriarch as a flood, once in a while a patriarch might forget to declare the lineage of the person being blessed. If that happens, he is authorized to lay his hands upon your head and give what is called an "addendum," in which he simply receives the revelation to know what tribe your blessings will come through. The addendum is not to be a second blessing—thus the patriarch would not traditionally add lots of other promises or warnings not stated in your original patriarchal blessing. The addendum is simply for the purpose of getting the revelation on your lineage. If you or the patriarch realize he has neglected to declare your lineage before the blessing has been transcribed, then the addendum would simply be incorporated into your original blessing. If it is not realized until later that the lineage is missing from the blessing, you can simply go to your bishop, get a recommend to receive an inspired addendum, and then make an appointment with the patriarch to receive this portion of your blessing by the laying on of hands.

—29—

What Blessings, Admonitions, or Warnings Did Israel and Moses Pronounce upon Ephraim?

Shortly before his death, Israel (whose birth name was Jacob) gave a patriarchal blessing to each of his sons (Genesis 49). The prophetic nature of these blessings was indicated by Jacob himself, who said to his sons, "Gather yourselves together, *that I may tell you that which shall befall you* in the last days" (Genesis 49:1; emphasis added). Similarly, shortly before he died, Moses pronounced a blessing upon each of the tribes of Israel (Deuteronomy 33). Through the declaration of their lineage, the blessings and warnings given to each of the tribes (by Jacob and Moses) are technically also pronounced upon all who receive their patriarchal blessing. Thus, the promises made to Ephraim are extended to all Ephraimites, the promises made to Levi are extended to all Levites, the promises made to Reuben are extended to all Rubenites, etc. When the stake patriarch declares your lineage, he is also renewing with you those blessings and warnings given to the father of your tribe.

In this section, and the twelve that follow, we will examine the blessings given to each of the tribal heads and how those blessings apply to their descendants (you and me) today. Just as it takes all twelve oxen to hold up the baptismal font in the temple, so also, each of the tribes of Israel has a role to play in accomplishing God's great latter-day work.[1]

Out of all of the tribes of Israel, Ephraim's blessing is the easiest to understand, in part because it is the longest and clearest and partially because latter-day prophets have spoken so clearly regarding the mission of the descendants of Ephraim.

President Boyd K. Packer (1924–2015), former President of the Quorum of the Twelve Apostles, indicated that Ephraim is "the tribe to which has been committed the leadership of the Latter-day work."[2] It is Ephraim's primary responsibility to "spearhead the great missionary effort" of the last days[3]—through which is brought to pass the "gathering of Israel." Members of the house of Israel are "gathered in" when they accept the restored gospel and then enter into (and keep) sacred covenants. Part of that process is the receipt of their patriarchal blessing, in which they have their tribal lineage declared.[4] "Missionaries gather them. Patriarchs identify them."[5] Those of the tribe of Manasseh assist the Ephraimites in this sacred charge. Those whose lineage is *not* Ephraim or Manasseh still play a role in the gathering. They act as "forerunners" for those of their own tribes.[6] While it is the "responsibility assigned to all Israel . . . to gather the lost of Israel and the elect of God and lead them back to Him,"[7] nevertheless, Ephraim has the leadership role in this work and has been called be the primary gatherer of scattered Israel.

The blessings pronounced upon Ephraim and his descendants (by Jacob) were actually given to his father, Joseph, but were then inherited by Ephraim—because he received his father's birthright. The content of Ephraim's two prophetic blessings (one from Jacob and the other from Moses) is as follows:

Israel's Blessing upon Ephraim	*Moses's Blessing upon the Tribe of Ephraim*
Ephraim, through Joseph, "is a fruitful bough, even a fruitful bough by a well; whose branches run over the wall: the archers have sorely grieved him, and shot at him, and hated him: but his bow abode in strength, and the arms of his hands were made strong by the hands of the mighty God of Jacob; (from thence is the shepherd, the stone of Israel:) even by the God of thy father, who shall help thee; and by the Almighty, who shall bless thee with blessings of heaven above, blessings of the deep that lieth under, blessings of the breasts, and of the womb: the blessings of thy father have prevailed above the blessings of my progenitors unto the utmost bound of the everlasting hills: they shall be on the head of Joseph, and on the crown of the head of him that was separate from his brethren." *Genesis 49:22–26*	"And of Joseph he said, Blessed of the Lord be his land, for the precious things of heaven, for the dew, and for the deep that coucheth beneath, and for the precious fruits brought forth by the sun, and for the precious things put forth by the moon, and for the chief things of the ancient mountains, and for the precious things of the lasting hills, and for the precious things of the earth and fulness thereof, and for the good will of him that dwelt in the bush: let the blessing come upon the head of Joseph, and upon the top of the head of him that was separated from his brethren. His glory is like the firstling of his bullock, and his horns are like the horns of unicorns: with them he shall push the people together to the ends of the earth: and they are the ten thousands of Ephraim, and they are the thousands of Manasseh." *Deuteronomy 33:13–17*

There are a number of components to Joseph's blessing—things which would be fulfilled through Ephraim and his posterity.

He was promised that he would be "a fruitful bough, even a fruitful bough by a well." The imagery is that of a tree that is planted by a spring that, because of its abundance of water, would grow large and fast. The Lord is promising the descendants of Joseph (through Ephraim) that they would be large and fruitful—and that is exactly what the Ephraimites within the Church are. They are the most numerous of the tribes, and their lives—along with the conversions to the gospel that they bring—are the fruits of this promise.

It is said that Ephraim will "push the people together to the ends of the earth"—much like how an animal uses its horns to push something. This has been understood to mean that, in their role of gathering, the Ephraimites would be powerful (as the symbol of the horn suggests), and through their powerful faith and testimonies, they would successfully push many toward the truth. Significantly, the ancient symbol of the tribe of Ephraim was the ox—which harmonizes well with the image of the animal pushing people to the gospel. More particularly, just as the temple baptismal fonts rest upon the back of oxen, the majority of the work of gathering scattered Israel rests upon the shoulders of the tribe of Ephraim.[8]

Joseph is promised that his "branches" would "run over the wall." This has been understood to mean that his descendants would leave the boundaries of Canaan for a new land—a promised land. Of course, anciently Ephraim's posterity did so. Moreover, today, many descendants of Ephraim leave their homelands to seek a new land—a promised land—in the "everlasting hills" or mountains. One of the primary responsibilities of the Ephraimites is to gather people into the Church and, while they may not bring them all to the mountains of Utah, they certainly draw them all to the "mountain of the Lord's house"—which is the holy temple (Isaiah 2:2).

The Ephraimites were promised that, though they would be persecuted and "hated," the "mighty God of Jacob" would help and protect them. Unquestionably, since the very beginning of the Restoration when the Prophet Joseph Smith—himself an Ephraimite—initially shared his First Vision, the enemies of the Church have hated and persecuted those who have aligned themselves with the restored gospel. Nevertheless, God has protected and moved forward His work, in spite of its enemies.

Through Joseph's blessing, Ephraim is told that he would be "separate from his brethren" and that the "blessings of thy father have prevailed above the blessings of my progenitors." This has traditionally been understood to mean that Ephraim and his posterity would be singled out as the chosen tribe—assigned the leadership role in God's work of gathering covenant Israel. The blessing of Joseph (Ephraim's father) should have fallen upon Reuben, but, because of sin, Ephraim would "prevail," receiving the birthright instead of his older brother.

God promised Ephraim that "thy brethren shall bow down unto thee, from generation to generation, unto the fruit of thy loins forever" (Joseph Smith Translation, Genesis 48:10). Because the Ephraimites would have the chief responsibility of doing missionary work and temple work, all other tribes would ultimately bow to them in order to receive their blessings at Ephraim's hands.

"The blessing and mission of the lineage of Joseph"—as found in his descendants, the Ephraimites—"is to bring salvation to his brethren."[9] (See Zechariah 10:6–10; D&C 133:25–26, 29–35.)

Finally, the Ephraimites were promised that "the precious things of heaven" would "come upon" them (through their faithfulness). Indeed, in the two blessings pronounced (by Jacob and Moses) upon Ephraim and his descendants, God offers the best blessings heaven and earth have to offer. God's choicest promises are listed as the inheritance of any Ephraimite that keeps his or her covenants with the Lord.

If you are of the tribe of Ephraim, perhaps this blessing upon your lineage is an invitation—even a command—to be a missionary and leader in the Church. It may be a call to you to reach out to others and to be active in temple work. This blessing upon your tribe might be perceived as a warning to you to not fear man but to trust God in all things and to be willing to be taken by God wherever He chooses to take you.

Notes

1. See Gayla Wise, *The Power of Your Patriarchal Blessing* (Provo, UT: Spring Creek, 2007), 46.
2. Boyd K. Packer, "The Stake Patriarch," *Ensign*, November 2002, 44.
3. John L. Lund, *Understanding Your Patriarchal Blessing* (Orem, UT: Noble Publishing, 1980), 40.
4. See Wise, *The Power of Your Patriarchal Blessing*, viii.
5. Wise, *The Power of Your Patriarchal Blessing*, 45.
6. Lund, *Understanding Your Patriarchal Blessing*, 42–43.
7. Garry H. Boyle, *A Loving Letter from God: Your Patriarchal Blessing* (Springville, UT: Cedar Fort, 2015), 41.
8. I express appreciation to Brother David T. Durfey, a stake patriarch, for this valuable insight.
9. Wise, *The Power of Your Patriarchal Blessing*, 59.

—30—

What Blessings, Admonitions, or Warnings Did Israel and Moses Pronounce upon Manasseh?

As with Ephraim, the blessings pronounced (by Jacob and Moses) upon Manasseh and his descendants were actually given to his father, Joseph, but were then inherited by Manasseh—as he and his younger brother, Ephraim, were favored by their grandfather because of their deep love for their father. The content of Manasseh's two prophetic blessings is the same as those of Ephraim and are as follows:

Israel's Blessing upon Manasseh	Moses's Blessing upon the Tribe of Manasseh
Manasseh, through Joseph, "is a fruitful bough, even a fruitful bough by a well; whose branches run over the wall: the archers have sorely grieved him, and shot at him, and hated him: but his bow abode in strength, and the arms of his hands were made strong by the hands of the mighty God of Jacob; (from thence is the shepherd, the stone of Israel:) even by the God of thy father, who shall help thee; and by the Almighty, who shall bless thee with blessings of heaven above, blessings of the deep that lieth under, blessings of the breasts, and of the womb: the blessings of thy father have prevailed above the blessings of my progenitors unto the utmost bound of the everlasting hills: they shall be on the head of Joseph, and on the crown of the head of him that was separate from his brethren." *Genesis 49:22–26*	"And of Joseph he said, Blessed of the Lord be his land, for the precious things of heaven, for the dew, and for the deep that coucheth beneath, and for the precious fruits brought forth by the sun, and for the precious things put forth by the moon, and for the chief things of the ancient mountains, and for the precious things of the lasting hills, and for the precious things of the earth and fulness thereof, and for the good will of him that dwelt in the bush: let the blessing come upon the head of Joseph, and upon the top of the head of him that was separated from his brethren. His glory is like the firstling of his bullock, and his horns are like the horns of unicorns: with them he shall push the people together to the ends of the earth: and they are the ten thousands of Ephraim, and they are the thousands of Manasseh." *Deuteronomy 33:13–17*

Like Ephraim, God promised Manasseh and his descendants that they would be "a fruitful bough, even a fruitful bough by a well." In other words, this tribe is expected to grow large and at a faster rate than most of the other tribes of Israel. And such has been the case; Manassites are currently the second largest tribe in the Church, and they are joining in large numbers—particularly in places like Latin America. The "fruits" of Manasseh are evident in the way they live their lives and in the propensity of many of that tribe to readily believe the gospel when they hear it.

Joseph was promised that his "branches" would "run over the wall." As we noted above, this has been understood to mean that his descendants would leave the boundaries of Canaan for a new land—a promised land. Evidence that the tribe of Manasseh did so is to be found in the story of Lehi, who was of the tribe of Manasseh. The exodus that he led is a literal fulfillment of Israel's promise to Joseph's son, Manasseh. In addition, since one of the primary responsibilities of those who are of the tribe of Manasseh is to assist the Ephraimites in gathering people into the Church, today Manassites fulfill this part of their blessing as they do missionary work—whether as a full-time missionary or as a member missionary. They are to "push" as many as will hear the message of the Restoration toward the baptismal font and toward the holy temple. Consequently, God promised Manasseh "thy brethren shall bow down unto thee, from generation to generation, unto the fruit of thy loins forever" (Joseph Smith Translation, Genesis 48:10). As the Manassites fulfill their responsibility of doing missionary work and temple work, all other tribes will ultimately bow to them in order to receive their blessings at their hands and at the hands of the Ephraimites.

As they do their sacred work on behalf of God, the Manassites are promised that they will be protected—even though many would loathe them for their faith in the restored gospel. Nevertheless, God will fight their battles, because He will see their love for and devotion to Him.

Finally, like the Ephraimites, those of the tribe of Manasseh were promised that "the precious things of heaven" would "come upon" them. As inheritors of a chosen status, God offers the best blessings heaven and earth have to offer to His sons and daughters in the tribe of Manasseh. All they must do is keep their covenants.

If you are of the tribe of Manasseh, this blessing upon your lineage could be seen as a call to you to be heavily engaged in the four-fold mission of the Church: perfecting the Saints, proclaiming the gospel, redeeming the dead, and caring for the poor and the needy. The blessing can be understood as a call and command to believe in God and to trust in His promises—even in the face of opposition. It appears to offer a promise that, in all that you faithfully do in the name of the Lord, you will be protected and helped until you have finished your mission upon the earth.

—31—

What Blessings, Admonitions, or Warnings Did Israel and Moses Pronounce upon Reuben?

REUBEN INITIALLY HAD THE BIRTHRIGHT THAT WOULD EVENTU-ally go to Ephraim. However, he lost it through his personal sins. Nevertheless, God still had a blessing for him—and for his righteous descendants. The blessings that Jacob and Moses pronounced upon Reuben and his lineal descendants are as follows:

Israel's Blessing upon Reuben	Moses's Blessing upon the Tribe of Reuben
"Reuben, thou art my firstborn, my might, and the beginning of my strength, the excellency of dignity, and the excellency of power: Unstable as water, thou shalt not excel; because thou wentest up to thy father's bed; then defiledst thou it: he went up to my couch." *Genesis 49:3–4*	"Let Reuben live, and not die; and let not his men be few." *Deuteronomy 33:6*

At first reading, this may not appear to be a blessing; rather, it may sound like a chastisement. However, we should keep in mind that one of the purposes of a patriarchal blessing is to warn the blessing's recipient of areas in his or her life that need attention. It is for this reason that Reuben is warned of being "unstable" and is told to be the "excellency of dignity," or, as we would say today, a righteous example and a credit to his father. Though Reuben lost the birthright of the firstborn through sin, he is still encouraged to live faithfully after his mistake—and his posterity is warned to learn from their ancient father's poor choice.

In his blessing, Israel compares Reuben to water because, in Mosaic symbolism, water was often a symbol for chaos and instability. Water is not firm nor is it stable, but we, as followers of Christ, should be both. Water must be contained in order to retain its shape, otherwise it runs everywhere. Those who have made covenants with God should exhibit self-control rather than having to be commanded in all things (D&C 58:26). Water molds to whatever container it is placed in, yet we, as God's covenant people, are not to conform to the world—but only to the ways and will of God. Regarding water's instability, one commentator pointed out, "Any breeze can ruffle its surface."[1] However, as true disciples of Jesus Christ, we must not allow ourselves to be moved every time a new societal trend or wind blows.

In his patriarchal blessing, Reuben is also told, "Thou shalt not excel." One author suggested, "The birthright had been given to the son of Joseph, the eleventh born of Israel, and Reuben was not to try to take it back. . . . The story of Reuben . . . reminds us that blessings can be forever lost by unrighteous conduct."[2] Again, what may feel like a punishment upon Reuben is actually a blessing to his posterity, who are warned to be cautious so that *they* do not lose the remarkable promises and gifts God wishes to bestow upon *them*.

Reuben's blessing also highlights our ability to repent if we make a mistake. Thus, Moses blesses him that he will "live, and not die"—and his posterity will not be small. Thus, a very positive aspect is added to his blessing; any who repent *can* be forgiven!

To Reuben's credit, it will be remembered that he was the only one of Joseph's brothers who stood up for him. Reuben was courageous, confronting his envious brothers, insisting that they not kill Joseph (Genesis 37:21). As the firstborn son, Reuben felt that he had every reason to be angry with Joseph—who inherited his birthright. However, he chose to act benevolently instead when Joseph was in a precarious situation. "Let us honor Reuben for his benevolence toward the brother who received the birthright instead."[3] And let us follow his example, standing up for all whom we perceive to be threatened or in danger.

If you are of the lineage of Reuben, this blessing upon your tribe might be seen as a command to live in such a way that you bring credit to your earthly and heavenly parents. It is potentially an invitation to be aware of—and cautious about—those areas in your life where you are a bit "unstable," so that Satan doesn't get his proverbial "foot in the door" and cause you to lose your eternal inheritance (or birthright) as Reuben lost his. This blessing is a reminder to be stable in all that you do and a warning that you should never seek to conform to the ways of the world but, instead, follow the ways of the Lord. It is also a reminder of God's love for the Reubenites and of their ability to repent when they make bad choices—even after they have committed serious sins, as Reuben had. Finally, Reuben's patriarchal blessings (through Jacob and Moses) are also invitations to all of his descendants to have the courage to come to the defense of others—even their perceived enemies.

Notes

1. J. H. Hertz, *The Pentateuch and Haftorahs*, 2nd ed. (London: Soncino Press, 1962), 183.
2. John L. Lund, *Understanding Your Patriarchal Blessing* (Orem, UT: Noble Publishing, 1980), 4–5.
3. Gayla Wise, *The Power of Your Patriarchal Blessing* (Provo, UT: Spring Creek, 2007), 48–49.

—32—

What Blessings, Admonitions, or Warnings Did Israel and Moses Pronounce upon Simeon?

ACCORDING TO THE BIBLE, ISRAEL PRONOUNCED A SINGULAR BLESSing upon Simeon and his brother Levi—largely because their choices had been similar and, thus, God's warning to them was similar. The blessing that Jacob pronounced upon Simeon and his lineal descendants is as follows:

Israel's Blessing upon Simeon	Moses's Blessing upon the Tribe of Simeon
"Simeon and Levi are brethren; instruments of cruelty are in their habitations. O my soul, come not thou into their secret; unto their assembly, mine honour, be not thou united: for in their anger they slew a man, and in their selfwill they digged down a wall. Cursed be their anger, for it was fierce; and their wrath, for it was cruel: I will divide them in Jacob, and scatter them in Israel." *Genesis 49:5–7*	Moses pronounced no blessing on the tribe of Simeon, most likely because—for the most part—over time they merged with the tribe of Judah, seldom distinguishing themselves from the Judahites.[1]

In his blessing upon Simeon, Jacob reminds his son of his horrific and sinful actions, where he slew (with his brother) "all the males" of the Shechemites (Genesis 34:25) because one man—"Shechem the son of Hamor the Hivite" (Genesis 34:2)—had defiled Simeon's sister, Dinah. While the death of Shechem may have been justified because he raped a girl, the death of all other men in the city was not justified. One commentator suggested that, though Jacob was upset at Simeon for the terrible thing he had done, the patriarch (through this blessing) "is saying that [Simeon] possessed the attribute of kingship" because he was acting out of love for his sister.[2] Of course, the message to all Simeonites is to never act out of anger, as Simeon and his brother did. When we act out of anger, we seldom act objectively.

One scholar suggested that we should not be caught up in the negative part of Simeon's blessing but, instead, "remember also his good qualities, shown in his attitudes and actions toward [his brother] Joseph."[3] You may recall that it was Simeon who was the hostage who remained behind in Egypt while the other brothers went to get Benjamin (Genesis 42:19, 24, 36; Genesis 43:23). This part of the blessing is an invitation to any of Simeon's tribe to look out for others and to be willing to put others before ourselves. This is good counsel to any Simeonite who is a spouse or parent. As you place your spouse or children before yourself, God will bless you and them—as He did Simeon and Benjamin.

It has been pointed out that, "From the tribe of Simeon come the scribes."[4] While, by New Testament times, the scribes were often associated with hypocrisy, in actuality, the scribes were originally individuals who dedicated their lives to God and to an intense study of His word (see Ezra 7:6, 10–12; Nehemiah 8:1, 4, 9, 13). Thus, for descendants of Simeon, being a member of this tribe is an invitation to study and know the scriptures and to teach their content to others.

One commentator pointed out that Simeon's "descendants will be among the one hundred forty-four thousand" whom the Apostle John saw as receiving exaltation in the Celestial kingdom of God.[5] Thus, to be a member of the tribe of Simeon and to keep one's covenants means a promise of eternal life.

If you are of the lineage of Simeon, this blessing upon your tribe is a reminder that none of us should ever act in cruel ways; nor should we ever act out of anger. This blessing is a reminder to all Simeonites to put others first in their lives—even if that requires personal sacrifice. It serves as an invitation and admonition to learn and love the scriptures. Finally, this blessing promises that, as you chart a path for exaltation, you will ultimately be saved in the celestial kingdom of God.

Notes

1. See Earl S. Kalland, "Deuteronomy," in Frank E. Gaebelein, ed., *The Expositor's Bible Commentary*, 12 vols. (Grand Rapids, MI: Zondervan, 1976–1992), 3:221.
2. Ramban Nachmanides, *Commentary on the Torah*, 5 vols. (New York: Shilo Publishing House, 1971), 1:583.
3. Ellis T. Rasmussen, *A Latter-day Commentary on the Old Testament* (Salt Lake City, UT: Deseret Book, 1993), 79.
4. Ambrose, "The Patriarchs," 3:11–13, cited in Mark Sheridan, ed., *Ancient Christian Commentary on Scripture: Genesis 12–50* (Downers Grove, IL: InterVaristy Press, 2002), 323.
5. See Rasmussen, *A Latter-day Commentary on the Old Testament*, 79.

—33—

What Blessings, Admonitions, or Warnings Did Israel and Moses Pronounce upon Levi?

WHEREAS SIMEON RECEIVED NO BLESSING FROM MOSES, LEVI received one from both Israel and also from the great prophet of the Exodus. The blessings that Jacob and Moses pronounced upon Levi and his lineal descendants are as follows:

Israel's Blessing upon Levi	Moses's Blessing upon the Tribe of Levi
"Simeon and Levi are brethren; instruments of cruelty are in their habitations. O my soul, come not thou into their secret; unto their assembly, mine honour, be not thou united [don't let me become like them]: for in their anger they slew a man, and in their selfwill they digged down a wall. Cursed be their anger, for it was fierce; and their wrath, for it was cruel: I will divide them in Jacob, and scatter them in Israel." *Genesis 49:5–7*	"And of Levi he said, Let thy Thummim and thy Urim be with thy holy one, whom thou didst prove at Massah, and with whom thou didst strive at the waters of Meribah; who said unto his father and to his mother, I have not seen him; neither did he acknowledge his brethren, nor knew his own children: for they have observed thy word, and kept thy covenant. They shall teach Jacob thy judgments, and Israel thy law: they shall put incense before thee, and whole burnt sacrifice upon thine altar. Bless, Lord, his substance, and accept the work of his hands: smite through the loins of them that rise against him, and of them that hate him, that they rise not again." *Deuteronomy 33:8–11*

Like Simeon, Jacob chastises Levi for his appalling and sinful actions (slaying innocent men and children in his anger over his sister's rape). Though it has been suggested that Israel (through this blessing) was saying that Levi possessed "the attribute of kingship"[1]—because he was acting out of love for his sister—nevertheless, Jacob is still condemning his son's violent actions. Of course, "one's descendants are not impaired by ancestors' misdeeds."[2] Consequently, the sins of Levi are not answered upon his tribes' heads. Rather, the message to all Levites is to never act out of anger, as Levi and his brother did. When we act out of anger, we seldom act aright. Anger always clouds our judgment.

Evidence that God did not hold against the Levites the sin of their tribal father is found both in Moses's blessing upon the tribe and also the fact that they became the sole tribe of Israel that was allowed to hold the Aaronic Priesthood and administer the ordinances thereof throughout the remainder of the Old Testament. As one stake patriarch noted, "Descendants of Levi have a special calling because Levi's children were separated from the rest to act as spiritual ministrants, and . . . the Levities provided the ordinances and spiritual needs of the community."[3] Consequently, if you are of the tribe of Levi, you should feel called to priesthood service. For men, this means faithfully holding and serving in the offices and ordinances of the priesthood. For women, this means receiving the ordinances of the priesthood and serving faithfully in callings and in the holy temple. Whether male or female, it means that when we are set apart for our callings, we are given priesthood authority to act and serve as God would have us act and serve.[4] To be of the tribe of Levi is a calling to be a faithful servant in any capacity the Lord invites us to serve in. It is to be a servant and minister to others and to do so in the way that the Lord would—because you represent Him. The name *Levi* means "pledged," and the Levites "did the Lord's physical work on the earth for Him as He couldn't be here."[5] They were the original "temple workers," pledging themselves to God and His service.

In Moses's blessing upon Levi, it is evident that they are to be teachers to the other tribes of Israel. Of course, one cannot teach what one does not know. Thus, this blessing is a call to all Levites to learn the word of the Lord and to walk in His ways.

The command in Moses's blessing to Levi to "let thy Thummim and thy Urim be with the holy one" has been interpreted to mean

"Let thy divine revelation be of God."[6] In other words, just as the Levites followed Moses and Aaron when others fought against them (at Meribah), each descendant of Levi today should be fiercely loyal to the Lord's anointed prophets and apostles. As the Levites of old, so also modern members of that tribe have a divine commission to testify to the world that God's prophets are inspired and that all should follow their counsel and guidance.

It is believed that, in the last days—leading up to the return of Christ—those of the tribe of Levi will play a special role. Elder Bruce R. McConkie (1915–1985) of the Quorum of the Twelve Apostles explained, "Members of this tribe will again in this final dispensation offer their traditional sacrifices to the Lord as a part of the Restoration of all things."[7] Of course, one who is of the tribe of Levi would want to ever keep himself worthy for when that opportunity arises.

The office of Presiding Bishop "is a birthright office belonging to the tribe of Levi."[8] Of all of the tribes of Israel, only the Levites have an office of the priesthood belonging to it—and to it alone. While non-Levites have sat in that office during modern times, presumably, at some time in the not-so-distant future, a faithful son of Levi will be raised up by the Lord to inherit that office, which belongs to the children of Levi.

If you are of the lineage of Levi, this blessing upon your tribe might be seen is a call to be worthy of the ordinances of the priesthood—and to serve faithfully in them throughout your life. It is perceivably an invitation to use any assignment or calling you have in the Church for the salvation of others. Being a Levite can mean you should sacrifice for and serve God's other children—and live the life that Christ lived so that others will see His face in yours. Membership in this tribe should carry with it an expectation that you will always be loyal to the prophets. Moreover, this blessing offers a promise to all Levites that, as you are on His errand and faithful to your covenants, God will protect you from your enemies.

Notes

1. Ramban Nachmanides, *Commentary on the Torah*, five volumes (New York: Shilo Publishing House, 1971), 1:583.
2. Ellis T. Rasmussen, *A Latter-day Commentary on the Old Testament* (Salt Lake City, UT: Deseret Book, 1993), 79.
3. Garry H. Boyle, *A Loving Letter from God: Your Patriarchal Blessing* (Springville, UT: Cedar Fort, 2015), 139.
4. Dallin H. Oaks, "The Keys and Authority of the Priesthood," *Ensign*, May 2014, 49, 51.
5. Gayla Wise, *The Power of Your Patriarchal Blessing* (Provo, UT: Spring Creek, 2007), 51.
6. D. Kelly Ogden and Andrew C. Skinner, *Verse by Verse: The Old Testament Volume One—Genesis Through 2 Samuel, Psalms* (Salt Lake City, UT: Deseret Book, 2013), 323.
7. Bruce R. McConkie, *Mormon Doctrine*, 2nd ed. (Salt Lake City, UT: Bookcraft, 1979), 401.
8. John L. Lund, *Understanding Your Patriarchal Blessing* (Orem, UT: Noble Publishing, 1980), 45.

—34—

What Blessings, Admonitions, or Warnings Did Israel and Moses Pronounce upon Judah?

THE BLESSINGS THAT JACOB AND MOSES PRONOUNCED UPON JUDAH and his lineal descendants are as follows:

Israel's Blessing upon Judah	Moses's Blessing upon the Tribe of Judah
"Judah, thou art he whom thy brethren shall praise: thy hand shall be in the neck of thine enemies; thy father's children shall bow down before thee. Judah is a lion's whelp: from the prey, my son, thou art gone up: he stooped down, he couched as a lion, and as an old lion; who shall rouse him up? The sceptre shall not depart from Judah, nor a lawgiver from between his feet, until Shiloh come; and unto him shall the gathering of the people be. Binding his foal unto the vine, and his ass's colt unto the choice vine; he washed his garments in wine, and his clothes in the blood of grapes: his eyes shall be red with wine, and his teeth white with milk." *Genesis 49:8–12*	"And this is the blessing of Judah: and he said, Hear, Lord, the voice of Judah, and bring him unto his people: let his hands be sufficient for him; and be thou an help to him from his enemies." *Deuteronomy 33:7*

In many ways, Judah's blessing is messianic—meaning it predicts the coming of Christ. In 1 Chronicles 5:2, we read, "For Judah prevailed above his brethren, and of him came the chief ruler; but the birthright was Joseph's." This has been interpreted to mean that, while Joseph (through his sons, Ephraim and Manasseh) would hold the birthright, Judah's posterity would have as a member of its tribe, the Messiah—even Jesus the Christ.[1] And so it is, "those born through the lineage of Judah come through the line of the kings. They share heritage with the great King David and with the King of Kings, Jesus the Christ."[2] Could one ask for a more special designation than that?

Among the many messianic components of this blessing, we find these. Judah receives no rebuke—and the Messiah would never need rebuke from His Father. Judah's brethren would praise and bow down to him—and all shall praise the Holy One of Israel and bow down to Him. Judah would prevail over all his enemies—and none shall defeat Christ. Judah is as a lion's whelp (or cub), the lion being a symbol for leadership—and Christ is the leader of all; Lord of lords and King of kings. The declaration that the scepter shall not depart from Judah, nor the lawgiver leave until Shiloh comes, is a promise that, until Christ (Shiloh) is born into that tribe, it would preserve the royal lineage. The foal is a reminder of the colt upon which He would ride during His triumphal entry; the stain of the "blood of the grapes" is a reminder that—when Christ returns—He will be wearing blood red. Promise after promise in this blessing point to Judah as the chosen tribe to give birth to the Son of God—and with a calling to live lives which emulate Him.[3]

One author pointed out, "Judah . . . pleaded for Benjamin's freedom, saying, '. . . let [me] abide instead of the lad a bondman to my lord; and let the lad go.' (Gen. 44:20, 33.) So Judah offered to be a slave, even as he had once sold Joseph, to honor his pledge."[4] Curiously, as Judah offered to suffer in someone else's place, Jesus has offered to suffer in our place. For those who are members of this same tribe, therefore, you are invited to shoulder the burdens of others. Judah's actions are an invitation for his posterity to be selfless and self-sacrificing.

Moses's blessing upon Judah is really a prayer that God would help the tribe when confronted by its enemies. Of course, here is an example to all of this tribe; when you are in danger or in need, it is to God that you should turn. The arm of the flesh will often fail you, but the arm of God will always provide (2 Nephi 4:34–35).

In Doctrine and Covenants 133:35, we read, "And they also of the tribe of Judah, after their pain, shall be sanctified in holiness before the Lord, to dwell in his presence day and night, forever and ever." Here the Lord promises that, though Judah will suffer some pain as part of their mortal experience, the ultimate destiny of those who faithfully endure is to dwell eternally with God in the celestial kingdom. No more precious promise could one hope for.

If you are of the lineage of Judah, this blessing upon your tribe may suggest that leadership is native to those of your lineage. This blessing also promises protection, but it may additionally call you to be like the very One who will protect you—even Jesus the Christ. The blessing upon the tribe of Judah is void of any criticism because of Judah's faithfulness and, therefore, can be seen as a call to all within this tribe to live a life of strict obedience to God and His commandments. Because Judah is of the same blood as was Jesus, his tribe's members should live the same life as Jesus. Part of that life is becoming a selfless person, like unto your Savior.

Notes

1. See John L. Lund, *Understanding Your Patriarchal Blessing* (Orem, UT: Noble Publishing, 1980), 43–44.
2. Gayla Wise, *The Power of Your Patriarchal Blessing* (Provo, UT: Spring Creek, 2007), 51.
3. See D. Kelly Ogden and Andrew C. Skinner, *Verse by Verse: The Old Testament Volume One—Genesis Through 2 Samuel, Psalms* (Salt Lake City, UT: Deseret Book, 2013), 161–162.
4. Wise, *The Power of Your Patriarchal Blessing*, 52.

—35—

What Blessings, Admonitions, or Warnings Did Israel and Moses Pronounce upon Issachar?

THE BLESSINGS THAT JACOB AND MOSES PRONOUNCED UPON Issachar and his lineal descendants are as follows:

Israel's Blessing upon Issachar	Moses's Blessing upon the Tribe of Issachar
"Issachar is a strong ass couching down between two burdens: And he saw that rest was good, and the land that it was pleasant; and bowed his shoulder to bear, and became a servant unto tribute." *Genesis 49:14–15*	"Rejoice, . . . Issachar, in thy tents. They shall call the people unto the mountain; there they shall offer sacrifices of righteousness: for they shall suck of the abundance of the seas, and of treasures hid in the sand." *Deuteronomy 33:18–19*

Issachar was promised, as his inheritance, a land that was notoriously fruitful. The implication of this promise is that Issachar and his descendants would enjoy temporal blessings from the Lord. Certainly, many of those may be received during this mortal life. However, the most valued of all temporal blessings that God can bestow upon His faithful children would be an inheritance in the celestial kingdom.

Since the name Issachar means "there is a recompense," perhaps there is a promise in this for all those of the tribe of Issachar. The Prophet Joseph Smith once prophetically declared, "All your losses will be made up to you in the Resurrection, provided you continue faithful. By the vision of the Almighty I have seen it."[1] We may draw from this that those of this tribe, if they "continue faithful," will receive recompense for any sacrifices they are called upon to make here in mortality. What a great comfort that is.

The command that Issachar and his descendants "call the people unto the mountain; [where] there they shall offer sacrifices of righteousness" seems to point our minds to the "mountain of the Lord's house"—which is the holy temple (Isaiah 2:2). Thus, Issachar's tribe is called to speak of the temple and to teach about the temple, in the hopes that their hearers will embrace the message of the restored gospel and enter into the House of the Lord to "offer sacrifices of righteousness."

In 1 Chronicles 12:32, it suggests that the tribe of Issachar are those who have learned God's word and taught it. One commentary speaks of this tribe as "the student, the man of spirit."[2] The commission to those whose patriarchal blessing declares them to be of the tribe of Issachar seems obvious: study the scriptures and teach their content to others.

The description of Issachar as a "strong ass" has been understood as implying that this tribe would be blessed with "great physical power."[3] For some who are descendants of this tribe, this may mean great health and physical strength. For others, it likely implies the power of their work and words upon those to whom they minister.

If you are of the lineage of Issachar, this blessing upon your tribe may offer the promise of rich and abundant temporal blessings—whether in this life or the life to come. It may also stand as an invitation to you to exercise faith in God's promise that any sacrifice you are required to make here will be richly rewarded in the life to come. Finally, the blessing upon the tribe of Issachar can be seen as a call to be active in missionary work and temple work and active in studying, teaching, and testifying about both of those divine duties.

Notes

1. Joseph Smith, *Teachings of the Prophet Joseph Smith*, Joseph Fielding Smith, comp. (Salt Lake City, UT: Deseret Book, 1976), 296.
2. See J. H. Hertz, *The Pentateuch and Haftorahs*, 2nd ed. (London: Soncino Press, 1962), 913.
3. Hertz, *The Pentateuch and Haftorahs*, 185.

—36—

What Blessings, Admonitions, or Warnings Did Israel and Moses Pronounce upon Zebulun?

THE BLESSINGS THAT JACOB AND MOSES PRONOUNCED UPON Zebulun and his lineal descendants are as follows:

Israel's Blessing upon Zebulun	Moses's Blessing upon the Tribe of Zebulun
"Zebulun shall dwell at the haven of the sea; and he shall be for an haven of ships; and his border shall be unto Zidon." *Genesis 49:13*	"And of Zebulun he said, Rejoice, Zebulun, in thy going out . . . . They shall call the people unto the mountain; there they shall offer sacrifices of righteousness: for they shall suck of the abundance of the seas, and of treasures hid in the sand." *Deuteronomy 33:18–19*

Both Jacob and Moses bless Zebulun and his descendants with promises associated with the sea. Moses articulates it best when he says they will inherit the "abundance of the seas" and the "treasures hid in the sand." One commentator explained this promise, saying that those of the tribe of Zebulun are here "foreseen enjoying their homes and surroundings, and with good reason: their settlement would be in the choice valley of Jezreel, with good water from surrounding mountains, good soil, and a river that emptied into Israel's only natural harbor."[1] By application, those of this tribe today may have access to some of the choice temporal blessings of this earth.

Should the members of this tribe receive the wealth that the Lord has suggested could be available to those of their lineage, what should they do with it? The *Good News Bible* translation of this verse clarifies what God expects of them. "May Zebulun be prosperous in their trade. . . . They [should] invite foreigners to their mountain and offer the right sacrifices there" (GNB Deuteronomy 33:18–19). Mountains are standard symbols for the holy temple. Here we are told that Zebulun may be prosperous, but with that wealth, they should build the kingdom. They should invite "foreigners"—perhaps those who are foreign to the gospel or who are nonmembers—to come to the temple and participate in the "right" or acceptable ordinances of the Lord.[2] Thus, Zebulun is to be consecrated to the Lord. They are to use whatever God blesses them with to build the kingdom and to bring others to it. They are to use the temple and its great promises of eternal families and eternal life as a missionary tool in drawing others to Christ and His Church. The Hebrew name Zebulun means "exalted" (or "exalted abode"),[3] and as members of this tribe are faithful to the commission given them in this blessing, they will surely be exalted in the celestial kingdom.

Jacob promises Zebulun and his descendants that they shall "dwell at the haven of the sea; and . . . shall be for an haven of ships." The early Christians interpreted this as a commission to this tribe to help those who struggled with sin to make their way back to the Church and back to Christ. The Roman theologian Hippolytus (AD 170–235) explained, "Through Zebulun [Jacob] has metaphorically foretold the pagan nations"—those who were not members of the Church—"who live now in the world . . . and are tormented by the storm of temptations as if they were in the sea. Therefore they . . . look for refuge in harbors, that is, in churches."[4] The Italian theologian Ambrose (AD 337–397) explained, "Opening its arms, [Zebulun] calls into the lap of its tranquility those who are in danger and shows them a trusty place of anchorage."[5] In other words, if you are of the tribe of Zebulun, you should be looking out for those who are steeped in sin, for those whose lives resemble a ship in a storm, being tossed about and at risk of sinking. You should guide those whom you meet, who are in such a spiritual state, into the harbors of the restored gospel, where they can find refuge from the storms of life.

If you are of the lineage of Zebulun, this blessing upon your tribe cam be seen as an invitation to use your wealth to build God's kingdom. It is perceivably a commission to look for those who are struggling with their faith or who are steeped in sin and to encourage them to come to Church, where they will find strength and safely. Those of the tribe of Zebulun are encouraged here to use the temple as one of their tools in bringing others to Christ, for just as *Zebulun* means "exalted abode," drawing others to God's exalted abode (the holy temple) will place them on the path that leads to eternal life.

Notes

1. Ellis T. Rasmussen, *A Latter-day Commentary on the Old Testament* (Salt Lake City, UT: Deseret Book, 1993), 191.
2. See J. A. Thompson, *Tyndale Old Testament Commentaries: Deuteronomy* (Downers Grove, IL: Inter-Varsity Press, 1974), 314.
3. John H. Sailhamer, "Genesis," in Frank E. Gaebelein, ed., *The Expositor's Bible Commentary*, twelve volumes (Grand Rapids, MI: Zondervan, 1976–1992), 2:277.
4. Hippolytus, "The Blessing of the Patriarchs," 20, cited in Mark Sheridan, ed., *Ancient Christian Commentary on Scripture: Genesis 12–50* (Downers Grove, IL: InterVaristy Press, 2002), 335.
5. Ambrose, "The Patriarchs," 5:26, cited in *Ancient Christian Commentary on Scripture*, 335.

—37—

What Blessings, Admonitions, or Warnings Did Israel and Moses Pronounce upon Benjamin?

THE BLESSINGS THAT JACOB AND MOSES PRONOUNCED UPON Benjamin and his lineal descendants are as follows:

Israel's Blessing upon Benjamin	Moses's Blessing upon the Tribe of Benjamin
"Benjamin shall ravin as a wolf: in the morning he shall devour the prey, and at night he shall divide the spoil." *Genesis 49:27*	"And of Benjamin he said, The beloved of the Lord shall dwell in safety by him; and the Lord shall cover him all the day long, and he shall dwell between his shoulders." *Deuteronomy 33:12*

Moses calls Benjamin "the beloved of the Lord." God's love for those of this tribe is evident in their blessing, particularly in the promise that the Benjaminites would "dwell in safety by" God; the implication being that God would provide members of this tribe with the protection they needed to fulfill their earthly missions. Indeed, Moses describes God as carrying Benjamin "between his shoulders" like a father would carry his son or daughter upon his shoulders—an obvious symbol of love and caring.

Jacob refers to the Benjaminites as being like ravenous wolves who would devour their prey. Some have taken this to mean that those of this tribe would somehow be "fighters."[1] That should not necessarily be taken in a negative way. The tribe of Benjamin has had some rather famous members. For example, the Apostle Paul was a Benjaminite (Philippians 3:5). Paul was definitely a "fighter"—but, ultimately, a fighter in God's army, a fighter for the cause of truth.

One source said, "Paul . . . was a wolf to the wolves and snatched all souls away from the evil one."[2] Jacob's blessing upon this tribe may be an invitation to stand up for the truth—and to do so boldly and without fear. One commentator said, "Benjamin's blessing may predict his descendants' prevailing."[3] If the Benjaminites are faithful, God has promised in this blessing that He would help them prevail as they fought for the cause of Christ.

One source suggested of Benjamin, "He was not involved in that jealousy" that existed between his brothers. Rather, he sought to "bring people together." This same source suggested that those of the tribe of Benjamin may have the gift to be "peacemakers."[4]

If you are of the lineage of Benjamin, this blessing upon your tribe might be seen as a promise of divine protection and a sense of the Father's love for you. He will carry you in your most difficult times. This blessing can be understood as an invitation to never be "ashamed of the gospel of Christ" (Romans 1:16) but, instead, to boldly testify of the truth—even to your enemies. It may well be a call to be like Benjamin of old, who shunned things like jealously and pride.

Notes

1. See D. Kelly Ogden and Andrew C. Skinner, *Verse by Verse: The Old Testament Volume One—Genesis Through 2 Samuel, Psalms* (Salt Lake City, UT: Deseret Book, 2013), 164.
2. Ephrem the Syrian, "Commentary on Genesis," 43:11, cited in Mark Sheridan, ed., *Ancient Christian Commentary on Scripture: Genesis 12–50* (Downers Grove, IL: InterVaristy Press, 2002), 348.
3. Ellis T. Rasmussen, *A Latter-day Commentary on the Old Testament* (Salt Lake City, UT: Deseret Book, 1993), 81.
4. See Gayla Wise, *The Power of Your Patriarchal Blessing* (Provo, UT: Spring Creek, 2007), 67.

—38—

What Blessings, Admonitions, or Warnings Did Israel and Moses Pronounce upon Dan?

THE BLESSINGS THAT JACOB AND MOSES PRONOUNCED UPON DAN and his lineal descendants are as follows:

Israel's Blessing upon Dan	Moses's Blessing upon the Tribe of Dan
"Dan shall judge his people, as one of the tribes of Israel. Dan shall be a serpent by the way, an adder in the path, that biteth the horse heels, so that his rider shall fall backward. I have waited for thy salvation, O Lord." *Genesis 49:16–18*	"And of Dan he said, Dan is a lion's whelp: he shall leap from Bashan." *Deuteronomy 33:22*

The name *Dan* means literally "judge" but has also been interpreted as meaning "defend."[1] Thus, here Israel may be suggesting that the Danites would defend God's people. If this is the case, then the statement that Dan would be like a poisonous serpent (or adder)—that spooks the horse and his rider—makes sense. A snake defends his territory. Just as the tribe of Dan anciently stood as the "first line of defense"[2] against Israel's enemies, those of the tribe of Dan today should seek to be protectors of God's covenant people, of God's true Church. One text interpreted this blessing to mean that the Danites should be those who will fight for the truth.[3]

Because Dan is compared with a serpent, some have perceived this blessing as some kind of a curse upon the tribe of Dan. However, one early Christian source pointed out that the snake was often seen in ancient times as a symbol of Christ—not of Satan (see Numbers

21:4–8; Deuteronomy 8:15; 1 Nephi 17:41; Alma 33:18–22). The brass serpent that Moses raised up on his staff, and which symbolized Christ, caused the poison of the "fiery flying serpents" to have no effect upon those who were bitten.[4] Thus, this blessing upon the tribe of Dan may well be an invitation to them to also be healers of those who have been "bitten" by the devil's influence. As the Danites live Christlike lives, they can point those who are spiritually sick toward Christ—who has the power to heal us all.

Moses's promise that "Dan is a lion's whelp" that "shall leap from Bashan" has been interpreted to mean that Dan and his descendants would be agile and strong—filled with an adventurous spirit.[5] That being said, Jacob's phrase, "I have waited for thy salvation, O Lord," is sometimes translated, "I look for your deliverance, O Lord."[6] This has been interpreted to mean that the Danites would do well to trust not in their own strength but in the strength of the Lord. They may be agile and strong, but such gifts come only from God. As they trust in the Lord and keep Him as their companion, the Danites are promised "a future victory over their enemies."[7]

The promise that Dan would "leap" or "flee" from Bashan has been interpreted to mean that he would flee from "confusion."[8] Indeed, *Bashan* is sometimes translated as "serpent."[9] Thus, this certainly must be an invitation to all of Dan's descendants to flee from the devil and from all that provokes confusion—and to cling to the Spirit, which brings clarity and truth.

If you are of the lineage of Dan, this blessing upon your tribe might be taken as an invitation to be a defender of the faith, to protect the Church and its members from the adversary and his influence. Of course, you can only do this if you flee from temptation and sin. In this blessing, the Danites are perceivably invited to be healers of the spiritually sick. They can do this by pointing others to Christ's Atonement and ordinances, like the sacrament. The descendants of Dan are also reminded here of the importance of always relying upon the Lord—even if they have great strengths and talents of their own. Finally, this blessing upon those of the tribe of Dan suggests that many of them might be an adventurous people—as was their namesake.

Notes

1. See J. H. Hertz, *The Pentateuch and Haftorahs*, 2nd ed. (London: Soncino Press, 1962), 186.
2. D. Kelly Ogden and Andrew C. Skinner, *Verse by Verse: The Old Testament Volume One—Genesis Through 2 Samuel, Psalms* (Salt Lake City, UT: Deseret Book, 2013), 80.
3. See Gayla Wise, *The Power of Your Patriarchal Blessing* (Provo, UT: Spring Creek, 2007), 71.
4. See Ephrem the Syrian, "Commentary on Genesis," 43:6, cited in Mark Sheridan, ed., *Ancient Christian Commentary on Scripture: Genesis 12–50* (Downers Grove, IL: InterVaristy Press, 2002), 338.
5. See Hertz, *The Pentateuch and Haftorahs*, 913.
6. See John H. Sailhamer, "Genesis," in Frank E. Gaebelein, ed., *The Expositor's Bible Commentary*, 12 vols. (Grand Rapids, MI: Zondervan, 1976–1992), 2:278.
7. Sailhamer, "Genesis," in *The Expositor's Bible Commentary*, 2:278.
8. See Ambrose, "The Patriarchs," 7:34, cited in Joseph T. Lienhard, ed., *Ancient Christian Commentary on Scripture: Exodus, Leviticus, Numbers, Deuteronomy* (Downers Grove, IL: InterVarsity Press, 2001), 339.
9. See Ian Cairns, *Deuteronomy: Word and Presence* (Grand Rapids, MI: Eerdman's, 1992), 301.

—39—

What Blessings, Admonitions, or Warnings Did Israel and Moses Pronounce upon Naphtali?

THE BLESSINGS THAT JACOB AND MOSES PRONOUNCED UPON Naphtali and his lineal descendants are as follows:

Israel's Blessing upon Naphtali	Moses's Blessing upon the Tribe of Naphtali
"Naphtali is a hind let loose: he giveth goodly words." *Genesis 49:21*	"O Naphtali, satisfied with favour, and full with the blessing of the Lord: possess thou the west and the south." *Deuteronomy 33:23*

These two ancient blessings upon Naphtali and his posterity are brief, yet meaningful, as they highlight how members of this tribe can contribute to God's work.

The promise that Naphtali would be "a hind let loose" has been understood as an "image of swiftness and grace in movement."[1] A "hind" is a deer. Because of their swiftness, anciently, messages were often attached to their horns, and they would be sent with the communication to return to their original habitat. In this way, the king could receive speedy communication of news from other regions. Thus, Naphtali is here described as a swift and trusted bringer of good news—the ultimate good news being the gospel of Jesus Christ. Perhaps, in this blessing, there is a call to be a missionary.

On a related note, the phrase "he giveth goodly words" has been interpreted to mean that Naphtali would have great "speaking abilities," that members of the tribe would be "eloquent."[2] Thus, as the Naphtalites go about sharing the word of the Lord, they can do so endowed by God with great gifts of speaking and communicating the truth. This may imply that those of this tribe will be blessed with the gift of tongues.

Moses promises that those of this tribe, if they seek to live holy lives, will be favored of God and will be richly blessed by Him. Moses's blessing suggests that they would dwell in a fruitful land— or, in other words, would be blessed with prosperity.[3]

If you are of the lineage of Naphtali, this blessing upon your tribe could be taken as a command to share the good news. That "good news" surely includes sharing the truths of the gospel but may also extend to living a life of optimism, kindness, and love. Naphtali's blessing appears to promise rich and abundant gifts from God, including both monetary blessings and also remarkable gifts of the Spirit.

Notes

1. J. H. Hertz, *The Pentateuch and Haftorahs*, 2nd ed. (London: Soncino Press, 1962), 186.
2. See D. Kelly Ogden and Andrew C. Skinner, *Verse by Verse: The Old Testament Volume One—Genesis Through 2 Samuel, Psalms* (Salt Lake City, UT: Desert Book, 2013), 163; Hertz, *The Pentateuch and Haftorahs*, 186.
3. See Hertz, 914.

—40—

What Blessings, Admonitions, or Warnings Did Israel and Moses Pronounce upon Gad?

THE BLESSINGS THAT JACOB AND MOSES PRONOUNCED UPON GAD and his lineal descendants are as follows:

Israel's Blessing upon Gad	Moses's Blessing upon the Tribe of Gad
"Gad, a troop shall overcome him: but he shall overcome at the last." *Genesis 49:19*	"And of Gad he said, Blessed be he that enlargeth Gad: he dwelleth as a lion, and teareth the arm with the crown of the head. And he provided the first part for himself, because there, in a portion of the lawgiver, was he seated; and he came with the heads of the people, he executed the justice of the Lord, and his judgments with Israel." *Deuteronomy 33:20–21*

Jacob's blessing upon the tribe of Gad consists of a warning that Gad's enemies would attack him, but in the end, he would overcome them. Over the years, the Gadites successfully repelled the Ammonites, Moabites, and Aramaeans who repeatedly raided their borders.[1] Though they were strong, their strength was not entirely their own but was that of their "enlarger"—God.[2] Descendants of the tribe of Gad should expect, through their faith in God and faithfulness to Him, that they too will ultimately overcome their enemies.

Moses's blessing on Gad is difficult for some to understand. The prophet speaks of the ancient tribe of Gad as one that did its duty in fulfilling the commandments of God. Father in Heaven had decreed that Israel should inherit the land of Canaan. Gad, therefore, stepped up and did its part in the conquest of Western Palestine—tearing the arm and scalp of his enemies as he sought to execute God's justice and will. By application, those of the tribe of Gad should learn the will of the Lord and then apply all of their talent and strength to bringing it to pass. They should not sustain with their mouths only, but seek to join in the work with all of their "heart, might, mind and strength" (D&C 4:2).

The promise that Gad would select "the first part for himself," and would come "with the heads of the people," has been understood to mean that the Gadites would be natural leaders.[3]

If you are of the lineage of Gad, this blessing upon your tribe might be read as a promise that, should you be attacked (in any form) by those who are your enemies, God will help you to overcome. Father in Heaven may require that you bear the burdens of such attacks for a time, but in the end, He will exonerate the Gadites. These blessings upon the tribe of Gad may also be taken as a charge to faithfulness in their callings. God's words through Jacob and Moses may be taken as an invitation to the Gadites to learn their duty, and then to do it—giving their all on behalf of the Lord. As a lion is aggressive with its prey, the Gadites are invited to aggressively attack their work in the kingdom, thereby "bring[ing] to pass much righteousness" (D&C 58:27). The faithful Gadite will have many opportunities to serve in the kingdom, and some of those may involve leadership roles.

Notes

1. See J. H. Hertz, *The Pentateuch and Haftorahs*, 2nd ed. (London: Soncino Press, 1962), 186.
2. See Ian Cairns, *Deuteronomy: Word and Presence* (Grand Rapids, MI: Eerdman's, 1992), 300.
3. See Earl S. Kalland, "Deuteronomy," in Frank E. Gaebelein, ed., *The Expositor's Bible Commentary*, 12 vols. (Grand Rapids, MI: Zondervan, 1976–1992), 3:229.

—41—

What Blessings, Admonitions, or Warnings Did Israel and Moses Pronounce upon Asher?

THE BLESSINGS THAT JACOB AND MOSES PRONOUNCED UPON ASHER and his lineal descendants are as follows:

Israel's Blessing upon Asher	Moses's Blessing upon the Tribe of Asher
"Out of Asher his bread shall be fat, and he shall yield royal dainties." *Genesis 49:20*	"And of Asher he said, Let Asher be blessed with children; let him be acceptable to his brethren, and let him dip his foot in oil. Thy shoes shall be iron and brass; and as thy days, so shall thy strength be." *Deuteronomy 33:24–25*

The name *Asher* means "happy" or "blessed," and that certainly seems to describe what is promised to him and his descendants in his two patriarchal blessings. He is assured his life will be one of prosperity. He will enjoy "royal dainties"—or that which is fit for the table of a king. He is promised that, in many ways, his life will even be soft (as implied by his foot dipped in oil).[1] He is told that he will be "blessed with children" or—as the Hebrew reads—blessed "above the other children."[2] By this, it is implied that Asher's tribe will be one of the most blessed of all of the tribes of Israel.

In addition, Asher is promised that he (and his descendants) will be "acceptable to his brethren"—meaning, the Asherites will be respected and loved by their associates.

His shoes (or "bolts and locks," as the Hebrew says) will be strong, like iron, implying that Asher's home will be protected from invaders or enemies. Thus, God offers Asher physical protection.

If you are of the lineage of Asher, this blessing upon your tribe might be seen as a promise of potential abundant temporal blessings, and an invitation to be grateful as they come. It appears to be a promise that, if you are faithful, your life may be such that your associates will envy and respect you. It is certainly a reminder that, in all things, you should seek to be happy—because, in many ways, you may be blessed above that of many of your brothers and sisters. Perhaps it is also a warning that, if your life is in certain ways a life of ease, you must not allow yourself to become corrupted by that. Rather, you must work, contribute, and be generous with the abundance God has granted you.

Notes

1. See Earl S. Kalland, "Deuteronomy," in Frank E. Gaebelein, ed., *The Expositor's Bible Commentary*, 12 vols. (Grand Rapids, MI: Zondervan, 1976–1992), 3:231.
2. See J. A. Thompson, *Tyndale Old Testament Commentaries: Deuteronomy* (Downers Grove, IL: Inter-Varsity Press, 1974), 316.

—42—

What Does It Mean If My Blessing Says I Am "of Joseph," or "of Abraham," or That I Have "a Mission to the Lost Tribes," Instead of Declaring Me to Be of a Specific Tribe of Israel?

THOUGH NOT COMMON, SOME MEMBERS OF THE CHURCH DON'T have *any* of the blood of Israel in them. In a case such as that, the patriarch would not be prompted by the Spirit to declare them to be of a certain tribe. Consequently, he might simply state that they will receive their blessings "through Abraham," meaning that Abraham's bloodline posterity would bring them the gospel, they would be adopted into the house of Israel, and they would thus have a right to every blessing available to the faithful who were born with the blood of Israel in them.[1] As we have already noted, technically speaking—regardless of your physical lineage or bloodline—if you (through the Holy Ghost) gain a testimony that Jesus is the Christ and that the gospel has been restored, and if you act on that testimony by being baptized and receiving the gift of the Holy Ghost, then you are accounted as one of Abraham's seed (see Abraham 2:10; Galatians 3:14; Ephesians 3:6). As the Prophet Joseph taught, "The effect of the Holy Ghost upon a Gentile is to purge out the old blood & make him actually of the seed of Abraham. That man that has none of the blood of Abraham (naturally) must have a new creation by the Holy Ghost."[2]

As for those simply declared "of Joseph" in their patriarchal blessing, one author suggested this: "If your patriarchal blessing says

114

you are of Joseph and does not say either Ephraim or Manasseh, it is understood you were of Ephraim because Joseph stands at the head of the twelve tribes and Ephraim is the holder of the birthright position. Joseph and Ephraim become synonymous. . . . To be declared of Joseph only, is to be of the mission of Ephraim."[3]

While also not common, some people's blessings speak of a "special mission" to the "lost tribes of the house of Israel."[4] This has sometimes been interpreted as a mission to go to some hidden land in the north to discover these "lost tribes." In reality, a mission to the lost tribes simply means that you are to seek to convert people to the restored gospel of Jesus Christ. The lost tribes are only lost as to their eternal identity but *not* as it pertains to their physical location.[5] Thus, a call to the "lost tribes" simply means that you are to be an active missionary, helping those who don't realize they are children of God understand their eternal identity and their eternal potential.

Notes

1. See First Presidency letter, May 3, 2007.
2. Andrew F. Ehat and Lyndon W. Cook, *The Words of Joseph Smith: The Contemporary Accounts of the Nauvoo Discourses of the Prophet Joseph* (Provo, UT: Religious Studies Center, Brigham Young University, 1980), 4.
3. John L. Lund, *Understanding Your Patriarchal Blessing* (Orem, UT: Noble Publishing, 1980), 38.
4. See Lund, *Understanding Your Patriarchal Blessing*, 34.
5. See Alonzo L. Gaskill, *The Lost Language of Symbolism: An Essential Guide for Recognizing and Interpreting Symbols of the Gospel* (Salt Lake City, UT: Deseret Book, 2003), 162–166; Gala Wise, *The Power of Your Patriarchal Blessing* (Provo, UT: Spring Creek, 2007), 171.

Preparing for Your Patriarchal Blessing

"Prepare for the revelation which is to come."

Doctrine and Covenants 101:23

—43—

How Old Should I Be When I Receive My Patriarchal Blessing?

THERE IS NO SET AGE AT WHICH YOU SHOULD RECEIVE YOUR PATRI-archal blessing.[1] If you're prayerful, the Spirit will tell you when it is time. You should certainly wait until you are of sufficient age and maturity to understand the significance of a patriarchal bless-ing. Indeed, it is the bishop's responsibility to ascertain (during your interview) whether you are sufficiently spiritually mature to grasp the significance of such a blessing.[2] You should probably not receive your blessing until you are old enough to put some time into pre-paring yourself for that sacred day. One patriarch pointed out, "The maturity to receive a blessing is not about age; it is the strength of one's desire to know the will of God."[3] Converts to the Church should spend some time learning the basic doctrines of the restored gospel before they get their blessing—though, for most that should not take an extensive amount of time.

That being said, you should get your blessing early enough that most of your major life decisions are still ahead of you. Therefore, missionaries, for example, are strongly encouraged to get their patri-archal blessing before they enter the mission field. You would be wise to get yours before you start looking in earnest for your eternal com-panion. President James E. Faust (1920–2007), Second Counselor in the First Presidency, taught, "The patriarchal blessing is primarily a guide to the future, not an index to the past. Therefore, it is impor-tant that the recipient be young enough that many of the signifi-cant events of life are in the future."[4] Similarly, Sister Julie B. Beck

(b. 1954), former General Relief Society President of the Church, pointed out:

> You are in a season of your life when you are making some of your most important decisions. Because you are being bombarded with so many incorrect messages about who you are, you need some additional guidance. You can learn more about your life and mission on earth . . . by preparing to receive and then studying your patriarchal blessing. . . . I am glad I received my blessing before I was too heavily influenced by the confusing and incorrect messages in the world.[5]

It has been said that "fourteen- to twenty-four-year-olds find themselves living in the decade of important and life-determining decisions. During this period, it is helpful to have your blessing to guide you through most of that season."[6]

Eldred G. Smith (1907–2013), who served as Patriarch to the Church, told of giving a patriarchal blessing to a man who was in his nineties. The blessing was given, transcribed, and mailed to the man. However, before it arrived at the man's home, the elderly brother had passed away. Elder Smith noted that most of the blessing consisted of commendations for the way the man had lived his life, but it said little about his future—as the man was so elderly that he had little time left in mortality.[7] This story illustrates why getting our blessing early in our lives is of great advantage.

You should receive your blessing when you feel spiritually ready and worthy to receive it. You should not request a patriarchal blessing because your parents or grandparents are pressuring you to receive it. For your blessing to be the most effective and powerful in your life, it is best if you receive it only when you come to the point that you personally desire it—and are old enough to begin to understand it.[8] That desire and understanding can come at various ages.

Notes

1. Boyd K. Packer, "The Stake Patriarch," *Ensign*, November 2002, 43.
2. Packer, "The Stake Patriarch," 43.
3. Garry H. Boyle, *A Loving Letter from God: Your Patriarchal Blessing* (Springville, UT: Cedar Fort, 2015), 21.

4. James E. Faust, "Priesthood Blessings," *Ensign*, November 1995, 82.
5. Julie B. Beck, "You Have a Noble Birthright," *Ensign*, May 2006, 106.
6. Boyle, *A Loving Letter from God*, 147.
7. Eldred G. Smith, "Patriarchal Blessings," address given at the Salt Lake Institute of Religion, January 17, 1964, 6.
8. See Boyle, *A Loving Letter from God*, 148. See also Gayla Wise, *The Power of Your Patriarchal Blessing* (Provo, UT: Spring Creek, 2007), 9.

—44—

Are There Any Wrong Reasons for Getting a Patriarchal Blessing?

YOUR REASON FOR DESIRING A PATRIARCHAL BLESSING SHOULD BE A righteous one. If your sincere desire is to live a more righteous and Christ-centered life, your motivations for receiving your blessing are likely right and good. However, getting a patriarchal blessing because you are simply curious what the experience would be like, because you want to see the future, or because all of your friends are getting theirs are probably not good reasons to receive your blessing. It would be best to wait until you feel the whisperings of the Spirit urging you to receive it—and until you feel spiritually strong enough to live up to whatever blessings and warnings might be pronounced upon you.

In many ways, receiving a patriarchal blessing is like going on a mission. Serving a full-time mission is a wonderful and good thing to do. However, if you go on a mission for the wrong reasons— because your parents are pressuring you to go or because it's what all of your friends are doing—you will not be spiritually prepared for your call. If you go on a mission for the wrong reason, you'll not be effective as a missionary, and you may not have a good experience. So it is with your patriarchal blessing. It is a wonderful thing to want a blessing. However, if you are seeking one for the wrong reasons, you'll likely not have the powerful spiritual experience the Lord wants you to have, and you may hinder the Spirit during the blessing, preventing the patriarch from pronouncing some of the things he might say were you there for the right reasons and were you more spiritually prepared for the experience.

—45—

Do I Need Some Kind of Recommend to Get a Patriarchal Blessing?

In order to receive a patriarchal blessing, you will need to schedule an interview with your bishop. Call his executive secretary to make that appointment. In that interview, the bishop will ask you some questions about your personal worthiness, but he will also try to ascertain whether you are spiritually mature enough to receive such a blessing. The bishop will not be checking to see if you are *perfect*, only whether you are *trying* to keep the commandments and progressing in the gospel. Please remember, your bishop wants you to have your patriarchal blessing. He wants you to receive a recommend. He simply wants to make sure you do so worthily and when you are sufficiently prepared, because he knows it will be a more powerful experience for you if you are. So do not be afraid to approach him for a recommend or to talk to him about any struggles you're having with worthiness.

If for some reason you are receiving your patriarchal blessing by a patriarch who lives outside of your stake (you speak a different language than your stake patriarch, or your grandfather is a patriarch and will be giving you your blessing), you'll also need to have an interview with a member of your stake presidency before you can receive your blessing. If your circumstance requires this, call the stake executive secretary to make an appointment. The interview with your stake president will be very similar to your interview with your bishop. Both of these men love you and will be excited that you are preparing yourself to receive your patriarchal blessing.

After you receive your patriarchal blessing recommend, you—not your parents, spouse, or a family member—should call the patriarch to schedule the blessing. (One of the signs that you are mature enough to receive a blessing is that you are mature enough to schedule your own blessing appointment.)

—46—

What If I Don't Speak the Same Language as My Stake Patriarch?

WHERE POSSIBLE, THE CHURCH ENCOURAGES YOU TO RECEIVE your blessing in your native tongue. Thus, if your stake patriarch cannot speak a language you are fluent in, you are encouraged to request to receive your blessing from a patriarch that can give the blessing in a language you speak.

The prophets have strongly discouraged us from receiving our blessings in one language and then translating them into another language. A major reason for this is that it is often difficult to convey the exact meaning of the inspired words of the patriarch in a language other than the one he gave the blessing in. Your patriarch will feel very inspired in the words he speaks and in the specific words he chooses to use during the blessing. Indeed, when he types up the blessing, he will labor over the words used to ensure that they convey exactly what he was feeling at the time he gave you the blessing. Consequently, translating those words into another language—or worse, having someone else translate them—runs the risk of losing the inspired message God intended you to hear.

If you are *not* fluent in the language of your stake patriarch, the Church will allow you to receive your blessing from a patriarch who *is* fluent in your native tongue. You should go to your bishop and ask for his assistance in arranging this. While you will need an interview with both the bishop and a member of the stake presidency (in order to receive a blessing from a patriarch outside of your stake), they can help you to make the necessary arrangements to receive your blessing in your own language.

—47—

How Can I Best Prepare Myself to Receive My Patriarchal Blessing?

RECEIVING YOUR PATRIARCHAL BLESSING IS A ONCE-IN-A-LIFETIME experience. Thus, it is important that you prepare yourself so that the Spirit will be fully present during your blessing and so that the patriarch can receive what the Lord has in store for you. In an official Church publication on patriarchal blessings, it states, "Because of the spiritual nature of the blessing, we should do everything possible to lift ourselves from worldliness to a spiritual level equal to the occasion."[1]

Repent of the minor transgressions you commit from day to day and talk to your bishop about any major sins that you may not have confessed. He is a judge in Israel and can help you to ascertain if you are ready and worthy. If there are currently things in your life that disqualify you from receiving your blessing at this time, your bishop can help you to correct those so that you can be worthy to receive your blessing. If the spirit of revelation is to be present—so that the patriarch can be inspired—you need to be clean. The Lord doesn't require that you be perfect. However, He does expect you to be sincerely striving to be as clean as you can be. So, be open and honest with the Lord, your bishop, and yourself. If there are things in your life that would stifle the Spirit, take care of them so that the Spirit of the Lord can be unrestrained on the day you receive your blessing.

Pray for the patriarch that he can be inspired on the day he gives you your blessing. Remember, you are asking him to receive a revelation from God on your behalf. That is a remarkably sacred thing. The patriarch will need the Spirit to guide his words and open his mind to the revelations of heaven. Your sincere prayers will help him to make the connection with God that he will need in order to bless you.

In the months leading up to receiving your blessing, build your testimony through sincere prayer, contemplative scripture study, and regular temple attendance. Bear your testimony when the opportunity presents itself, and look for chances to serve others. As your testimony increases, your faith in revelation will increase, and your ability to feel the power of your patriarchal blessing will also be enhanced.

One of the ways to cultivate a desire for your blessing is by studying about patriarchal blessings and perhaps asking others about how their blessing has strengthened or blessed their life. Reading this book will help you, as will reading general conference talks on the subject of patriarchal blessings. (There are several mentioned in the notes of this book.)

Strive to be more obedient to God's commandments than you may have been in the past. Look for one or two things that you know you can *and should* do better at, and then work on improving those parts of your life. Obedience or submissiveness fosters humility, and your humility will allow the Spirit to speak more freely to you through the patriarch.

Do what you can to limit contention in your own life and family. If you are prone to argue with your siblings or your parents, practice controlling yourself and your emotions. Try to not let yourself get angry, and try to not be argumentative. Strive to be a peacemaker with your family and friends. One stake patriarch told me that, on the day of the blessing, he pulls aside the person who is to be blessed and asks, "Is today the right day for you to receive your patriarchal blessing? Has there been any contention today between you and your parents?" His reason for doing this is that, if there is unresolved contention, the Spirit may not be fully present—and that will certainly influence the content of the blessing.

Be cautious about the things you watch, read, or listen to in the weeks leading up to your blessing. You'll be surprised how easily some things we think are entertaining can offend the Spirit of the

Lord. Be sensitive to the promptings of the Holy Ghost. If it tells you to change the channel or station, do so immediately. The Lord will richly bless you if you will do this.

On the day that you actually receive your blessing, there are some additional things you can do to ensure that the Spirit of the Lord is unrestrained in your life and during your blessing.

First of all, have a prayerful attitude. We should certainly pray every day, multiple times each day. However, on this day, prayer may be even more important, because it will get your mind and heart prepared for what you are about to receive. If you are more prayerful than usual that day, you increase the likelihood that you will have a spiritual experience during your blessing. Again, pray for the patriarch that he can be inspired and that the stresses of life will not be upon him that day when he lays his hands upon your head and blesses you. Fasting is not required on the day you receive your blessing, but is an option that may help you to more fully feel the Spirit of the occasion.[2] Fasting is a form of sacrifice which Isaiah tells us increases the likelihood that God will hear and answer our prayers (see Isaiah 58:9).

When you go to receive your blessing, wear Sunday attire. This is a small thing, but it will invite the Spirit of the Lord—and it shows reverence for the sacred thing that is taking place.

The patriarch will spend a few minutes interviewing you prior to actually giving you your blessing. Avoid telling him things you would like for him to include in your blessing.[3] If you are spiritually mature enough to receive your blessing, then you will want the Lord to tell you what *He* wants you to hear; not what *you* want to hear. Listing for the patriarch things you would like for him to mention in the blessing shows a lack of faith on your part—and may hamper the spirit of revelation that the patriarch needs in order to give you an inspired blessing.

Remember, the patriarch will need to receive revelation that day on your behalf. Approach that day with the same spirit you would want with you if you were going to the temple.[4] If you are not spiritually prepared, it will make it harder for him to get the revelation needed—and this may affect the content of your blessing.[5] So do all you can to be worthy in the days and months leading up to receiving your patriarchal blessing. You need to be worthy—*not perfect*—but worthy when you receive it.

Notes

1. *Patriarchal Blessings* (Salt Lake City, UT: The Church of Jesus Christ of Latter-day Saints, 1979), 1.
2. Ezra Taft Benson, "To the Young Women of the Church," *Ensign*, November 1986, 82.
3. Garry H. Boyle, *A Loving Letter from God: Your Patriarchal Blessing* (Springville, UT: Cedar Fort, 2015), 28.
4. See Gayla Wise, *The Power of Your Patriarchal Blessing* (Provo, UT: Spring Creek, 2007), 15.
5. See Wise, *The Power of Your Patriarchal Blessing*, 12.

—48—

What Consequences Will Unworthiness Have upon My Blessing?

ALL BLESSINGS IN THE GOSPEL ARE CONTINGENT UPON OUR WORthiness. Doctrine and Covenants 130:20–21 states, "There is a law, irrevocably decreed in heaven before the foundations of this world, upon which all blessings are predicated—And when we obtain any blessing from God, it is by obedience to that law upon which it is predicated." That does not mean that God *only* blesses us when we are *perfectly* righteous. On the contrary, each of us receives blessings from God *every day of our lives.* If we have food to eat or clothes to wear, we are blessed. If we have family who loves us or friends who care for us, we are blessed. If we have a roof over our head or a job that helps provide for us, we are blessed. Consequently, none of us can say that God only blesses us when we are perfectly righteous. Even though we each sin *every day*, God blesses each of us in many ways *every day.* However, the more faithful we strive to be, the more access we will have to God's greatest blessings. When the patriarch places his hands upon our head and, by revelation, pronounces upon us the promises of God, in that instant we learn some of the higher blessings our Father in Heaven wishes to bestow upon us. These greater gifts and blessings are absolutely contingent upon our faith and faithfulness.

One stake patriarch shared his experience when trying to give a blessing to a young man who was not worthy to receive one. The patriarch said he felt very uncomfortable when the young man came in. The youth apparently sensed the patriarch's discomfort and confessed that he was not worthy to receive his blessing. The patriarch said, "I learned that when the words don't come, the influence of the Lord is not there."[1] Another patriarch told me that he knows he has given blessings to individuals who were not worthy to receive them. Of course, this hindered the Spirit during those blessings and, most likely, limited some of what the patriarch was able to say or promise in the blessing. It is so important to obtain your blessing when you are spiritually ready and worthy to receive it.

President James E. Faust (1920–2007), a member of the First Presidency, said, "If we are worthy, neither death nor the devil can deprive us of the blessings pronounced" in our patriarchal blessing.[2] However, the opposite is also true. "No blessing or promise will be fulfilled if the individual is not living a life worthy of that blessing. If a person begins to live unrighteously, his blessing can be a curse until proper and complete repentance is made. God will not be mocked."[3] Consequently, just as you need to be worthy *before* you receive your blessing, you also need to be worthy of the promises made to you *in* your blessing. If you fail to live up to the promises made to you by the Lord, you will most likely lose many of the blessings He has in store for you. Thus, it is imperative that you try to live faithful to your covenants.[4] President Brigham Young (1801–1877), second President of the Church, expressed concern that the members of the Church were living "far beneath" their "privileges" when it came to their right to be guided by revelation.[5] You and I should try hard, before and after receiving our blessing, to be worthy of all God has in store for us.

That being said, Sister Julie B. Beck (b. 1954), former General Relief Society President of the Church, reminded us:

> Sometimes young [people] think that because they have made mistakes, they are not worthy to receive a patriarchal blessing or that they have disqualified themselves from the blessing they have already been given. Remember, the foundational teaching of the Lord Jesus Christ is faith in Him and His power to atone for our sins. "Satan wants you to think that you cannot repent, but that is absolutely not true." [*For the Strength of Youth* (2001), 30.] When we take the sacrament each week, we commit to change our lives for the better. We should always be trying to become a new person who is more like our Savior Jesus Christ. The

Apostle Paul calls this "[walking] in newness of life." [Romans 6:4] If you have made serious mistakes that could disqualify you from your noble birthright, be willing to take your tears of sorrow to your bishop. He is your friend in the repentance process and is set apart to act as a judge here on earth in the place of the Savior, who is the Eternal Judge. Repentance is like a giant eraser, and it can erase permanent ink! It is not easy, but it is possible. [See *True to the Faith,* 132–35.] The Lord said, "He who has repented of his sins, the same is forgiven, and I, the Lord, remember them no more." [D&C 58:42][6]

Let us not deny the Atonement of Christ and its role in helping us obtain and retain the blessings promised to us in our patriarchal blessing. President James E. Faust said, "I humbly and prayerfully urge any who for any reason may not have lived so as to realize a fulfillment of the priesthood blessings pronounced upon them to so order their lives as to reclaim those blessings."[7] If we make mistakes—*and we all do*—we must not deny Christ's power to make things right. If we will change our heart and our behavior, Jesus can fix *anything* we have done wrong. Learn from your experiences and your mistakes and repent of any sins you are struggling with, but do not fixate on the past and things you cannot change. Do not dwell on sins you have repented of and overcome. Do not dwell on missed opportunities. Christ's Atonement is real, and as long as you are moving forward, God will have plenty of blessings in store for you in the future.

Notes

1. See Gayla Wise, *The Power of Your Patriarchal Blessing* (Provo, UT: Spring Creek, 2007), 85–86.
2. James E. Faust, "Priesthood Blessings," *Ensign*, November 1995, 82.
3. *Patriarchal Blessings* (Salt Lake City, UT: The Church of Jesus Christ of Latter-day Saints, 1979), 1.
4. Ed J. Pinegar and Richard J. Allen, *Your Patriarchal Blessing* (American Fork, UT: Covenant Communications, 2005), 85.
5. Brigham Young, *Discourse of Brigham Young*, John A. Widtsoe, comp. (Salt Lake City, UT: Bookcraft, 1998), 32.
6. Julie B. Beck, "You Have a Noble Birthright," *Ensign*, May 2006, 108.
7. James E. Faust, "Priesthood Blessings," 84.

—49—

Who Should Be in Attendance When I Receive My Patriarchal Blessing?

ONLY INVITE TO YOUR ACTUAL BLESSING THOSE WHOM YOU KNOW will add to the spirit of reverence that should prevail there. A spirit of flippancy or casualness will hinder the Holy Ghost and will thereby prevent the flow of revelation.

Usually it would be appropriate to have your parents with you when you receive your blessing—though, if your mom or dad are not members of the Church, you may want to be prayerful about whether they should be invited. If they are supportive of you being a member of the Church and of you receiving your blessing, then this may be a positive thing for them to witness. If they are somewhat antagonistic toward the Church or are unhappy that you have joined it, it may be best if they are not in attendance at your blessing. If you are prayerful about this, the Spirit will tell you what you should do.

Because we are a family-oriented Church, sometimes people want their whole extended family to be present when the blessing is given. However, because of the sacred nature of the event, it would be best to *not* invite large numbers of people to attend your blessing. Someone with a large family should not invite *all* of their siblings or their four grandparents to be in attendance when the patriarch pronounces the blessing because of the potential distraction it may cause for the patriarch and how that might hinder the Spirit which needs to be present. While there may be exceptions, generally speaking, this should not be a family event. Having too many people in attendance or young children in attendance can hinder the spirit of reverence that should prevail on such an occasion. In addition, because your blessing is a very personal and private revelation *just for you*, not many others should be allowed to know of its contents.

Generally speaking, a teenager should probably not invite his girlfriend or her boyfriend to be present when receiving a patriarchal blessing. Of course, a person who is the only member of the Church in their family may wish to have someone they are close to in attendance when they receive their blessing. If this is your situation, you should be prayerful about whom you invite. The Spirit of the Lord can direct you in this also.

—50—

What If I Am Afraid to Receive a Patriarchal Blessing?

MOST BISHOPS WILL TELL YOU THAT IT IS FAIRLY COMMON FOR young people to receive more than one recommend for their patriarchal blessing before they actually follow through and receive it.[1] I have known a number of youth who have gone through the effort to obtain their recommend to receive a patriarchal blessing and then *not* called the patriarch to schedule the appointment.

If you are afraid to get your blessing because of what the Lord may tell you in it—including expectations He may have of you—it is important to know that "His expectations of you are the same whether or not you receive the blessing to guide you in fulfilling them."[2] Just because you decide to not get the blessing doesn't change God's expectations of you. So, for example, if you're afraid to get your blessing because you worry that Heavenly Father will tell you that you need to serve a full-time mission, not getting the blessing doesn't remove your obligation to serve a mission. It just means that you're going to cruise through life somewhat uninformed. Of course, you are certainly welcome to try to do this on your own— spiritually blindfolded, as it were. However, the wiser approach would be to prepare yourself spiritually, and then go get the blessing so that you'll know what the Lord expects of you, and so that you'll have the help you need to fulfill those expectations.

If you are afraid to get your blessing, please remember, they are called patriarchal "blessings," not patriarchal "cursings." Your Heavenly Father is anxious to bless you. He is anxious for you to hear His voice (through the patriarch) and receive a blessing under

His hand. You have nothing to fear except your own lack of commitment to the Lord. Nevertheless, if you want to be good, and you want His help in being such, then you should *not* be afraid of what He will tell you in your blessing.

Notes

1. See Gayla Wise, *The Power of Your Patriarchal Blessing* (Provo, UT: Spring Creek, 2007), 13.
2. Wise, *The Power of Your Patriarchal Blessing*, 12.

—51—

Can I Make an Audio Recording of My Blessing When the Patriarch Gives It?

VOICE RECORDINGS OF PATRIARCHAL BLESSINGS ARE NOT PERMIT-ted. While it is true that the patriarch records it when he gives it, he only does so in order that it may be transcribed. However, once the blessing is typed up, the patriarch is required to erase the original voice recording. (Additionally, once he has given you a hard copy of your blessing and has placed the original copy of your blessing in his book of blessings—to be sent to Church headquarters—he is also required to destroy any electronic copies of your blessing.)

One reason why an audio recording of your blessing is not per-mitted is that the patriarch will have had certain impressions during the blessing. He will try to articulate those on the spot when he pronounces your blessing. However, when he creates the written transcript of your blessing, he may feel that the words he used at the time he blessed you did not adequately or fully express what the Spirit was telling him—and what he had tried to convey at the time. Thus, he may reword a sentence or two, or change a phrase here or there, to ensure that the written blessing accurately describes what the revelation he received for you meant. (It is important that you realize that the editing of your blessing happens just as much by the spirit of revelation as did the giving of your blessing. Your blessing is not final until you receive the written version from the patriarch.) If there were phrases used in the original blessing that were not what the patriarch meant or could be interpreted wrongly, having a recording of that might confuse or mislead you as to what the Lord was actually trying to say when He spoke (through the patriarch) to you. For this reason, audio recordings are not to be made.

Once You Have Received Your Patriarchal Blessing

———

"Live for the blessings you desire,
and you will obtain them."

President Brigham Young

In *Journal of Discourses*, 8:55.

—52—

How Long Will It Take for the Typed Copy of My Blessing to Arrive?

WHILE THERE IS NO SET TIME FOR WHEN A PATRIARCH HAS TO HAVE a copy of your blessing in the mail, generally speaking, patriarchs are encouraged to get the blessings transcribed and mailed (or delivered) as quickly as possible. It will typically not take more than a few weeks for the transcript of your blessing to arrive. However, remember that there is usually only one ordained patriarch for each stake. Sometimes the patriarch is very busy giving multiple blessings, each of which has to be reviewed, typed, and then mailed. At certain times of the year, such as when school has just gotten out, patriarchs can be quite busy giving blessings. Consequently, it is important to be patient, knowing that your patriarch will get your blessing to you as quickly as he is able.

—53—

What Are Some Ways to Get the Most out of My Patriarchal Blessing?

SPEAKING OF PATRIARCHAL BLESSINGS, PRESIDENT BRIGHAM Young (1801–1877), second President of the Church, counseled, "Live for the blessings you desire, and you will obtain them."[1] In other words, if you wish to see your blessing fulfilled—if you want to obtain each of the promises made to you therein—you must live in such a way as to make that happen. In this section, I will offer a number of ways in which you can use your blessing effectively so that it will be a powerful force in your life.

The first thing you should do is actually use it once you receive it. Too many members of the Church prepare themselves to obtain a patriarchal blessing but once it is received, seldom read or study it. President Gordon B. Hinckley (1910–2008), fifteenth President of the Church, told how he didn't read his patriarchal blessing until his mission.[2] Thus, in those early years, it wasn't a blessing to him. You should read your blessing *regularly* and *prayerfully*. President Joseph Fielding Smith (1876–1972), tenth President of the Church, said, "We should read them often to keep us from getting into byways and into forbidden paths."[3] As I noted earlier, most human beings will *never* have the chance to have a personal passage of scripture given just to them. This is a most sacred gift. Don't neglect it. Read it and reread it. Patriarchal blessings can be "lightning rods for revelation!"[4] Studying yours can provoke additional revelation not mentioned in the original blessing. Thus, President Monson (1927–2018) has said, "Your blessing is not to be folded neatly and tucked away. . . . Rather, it is to be read. It is to be loved. It is to be followed."[5] One stake patriarch suggested, "Do not wait for the powers of darkness to attack you. Study your patriarchal blessing and do even as Moroni, who built fortifications for his people in anticipation of future attacks. Let your patriarchal blessing become one of your armaments against the fiery darts of the adversary."[6] A patriarchal blessing is a gift from God. The Lord has said, "What doth it profit a man if a gift is bestowed upon him, and he receive not the gift?" (D&C 88:33). Are you using your gift?

Another thing you can do to make your blessing *a blessing in your life* is to have faith in the promises made to you through the patriarch. "Act as if it were a statement of reality, and it will become such through your faith, your diligence, and the heed that you give it."[7] Alonzo A. Hinckley (1870–1936) was President Gordon B. Hinckley's uncle and a member of the Quorum of the Twelve Apostles. In Alonzo's patriarchal blessing, he was promised, "If you continue to labor with the zeal you have started in with, you will be numbered with the Twelve Apostles of The Church of Jesus Christ of Latter-day Saints." Having received the blessing (as a young man), Alonzo thought to himself, "That's an impossibility." He said, "I became disappointed: I knew it couldn't be fulfilled: I lost my faith in the patriarch." He took the blessing, put it away, and never mentioned the promise to anyone—including his wife. However, many years later—on October 11, 1934—he was ordained an Apostle. Suddenly Elder Hinckley felt ashamed that he had neglected his blessing throughout his life. He said to his son, "I felt as if I would like to go down on my knees to Brother Ashman [the patriarch who pronounced the prophetic blessing] and ask his forgiveness for doubting, even for a moment, his inspiration as he gave me that blessing." Because he lacked the faith to believe in the promises in his blessing, he neglected it—never studying or pondering it throughout his life. He noted that, as a consequence of this neglect, "my blessing did not serve me as it should have done."[8] It is important that you believe the promises made to you—and that you live with all of your might to fulfill them. You should plead with Heavenly Father to bless you with the strength and foresight to be able to live up to the promises in your blessing—and to follow the counsel given to you in that sacred document.[9]

Another thing that is important to do is to "Avoid looking 'beyond the mark' (Jacob 4:14). You should avoid reading things into your blessing that are not there."[10] For example, one young woman justified marrying outside of the temple because her blessing said she would be "sealed" in the temple, but it didn't say she would be "married" in the temple. She had a non-LDS boyfriend that she very much wanted to marry. So, in order to justify marrying outside of the temple, she twisted the words of her blessing to mean something they did not.[11] In so doing, her blessing was not a blessing to her.

On a related note, you should remember that patriarchal blessings aren't necessarily in chronological order. As a singular illustration, if your blessing doesn't mention a mission until near the end of your blessing, don't assume that you should not serve a mission as a young man or young woman. Accept what the Lord has told you in your blessing, and don't try to twist it to make it say what you want it to say. Patriarchal blessings aren't the spiritual equivalent of an all-you-can-eat buffet. You can't pick and choose what you like in it and ignore the counsel or commands that you don't like. "If you are admonished to obey and then have an inclination to say, 'Well, but I won't do this or I won't do that,' you are setting aside the word of the Lord and forfeiting the blessings that come through obedience."[12] Your blessing is going to ask you to do some things that might not be what you would prefer. Do them anyway—and do them with all of your heart. "God is more interested in making you holy than popular. He is more interested in developing your character than making your life easy."[13] President Ezra Taft Benson (1899–1994), thirteenth President of the Church, taught, "Men and women who turn their lives over to God will discover that He can make a lot more out of their lives than they can."[14] Your patriarchal blessing is designed to help God make you great. Don't fight against that, or you will lose precious blessings.

In order to make convenient the regular reading of your blessing, put a copy of it in your scriptures or on your cell phone and read it during sacrament meeting as you prepare to take the sacrament—or after you've partaken. That is the perfect time to think about your life mission and to receive inspiration as to what the Lord needs you to do and become.

One young woman told me of how she made a recording of herself reading her patriarchal blessing, which she kept in a password-protected file on her cell phone. She would listen to it while she was driving, exercising, or as she lay in bed at night. Because she listened to it often, she found that she had largely memorized it. In times of temptation or discouragement, phrases from her blessing would come to her mind, protecting her and strengthening her.

You might want to consider creating a topical version of your patriarchal blessing. Hyrum G. Smith (1879–1912), general Patriarch to the Church, suggested that we should try to find the "keynote" or main theme of our blessing.[15] Similarly, Elder John A. Widtsoe (1872–1952) of the Quorum of the Twelve Apostles wrote, "Attention should be fixed upon the one great meaning of the blessing rather than upon particular statements."[16] A topical version of your blessing can help with this. Of course, not all patriarchal blessings have a singular theme; some will have several. However, the search for a theme will help you in your efforts to truly think about the content of your blessing and to discover what your life mission is. God expects us to put forth effort to discover our life's purpose.[17] Your patriarchal blessing is a key to the discovery and magnifying of that mission.[18]

On a similar note, "There may be a phrase or blessing" mentioned in your patriarchal blessing—or in the blessing of your spouse or one of your children—"that you may find is a good family theme."[19] Memorize it. Write it where you can see it. Perhaps make a plaque with the phrase or theme on it. Talk about it during family home evening. This can strengthen you and your family, and it is a reminder that God is aware of you and has a Fatherly concern for you, your spouse, and your children.

When you read your blessing, look for gifts of the Spirit that are mentioned therein. The gifts of the Spirit specifically promised to you in your blessing are keys to how God wants you to help build His kingdom here on the earth.[20] Therefore, if your blessing mentions specific gifts of the Spirit, you should read all you can about those gifts so that you can develop and use them to the fullest extent possible. Perhaps you might want to mark them in your scriptures in a color that you associate with your patriarchal blessing. Studying about them will enable you to be a better instrument in God's hands. "Often your spiritual gift is the key to your life's mission. . . . There are those who are waiting for you to share your gift. Do not make the Lord raise up someone else to do what you were sent to this earth to do."[21]

Because your blessing is personal scripture from God to you, it may be helpful for you to cross-reference the advice given to you in your blessing with the scriptures, teachings of the living prophets, and recent general conference talks.[22] For example, notice how the scriptures and the teachings of modern Church leaders have been incorporated into this sample paragraph from a patriarchal blessing:

> Dear brother, I bless you—as one who has received the Melchizedek Priesthood, even the Holy Priesthood after the Order of the Son of God [**D&C 107:3**]—that you will be the instrument through which God, your Father, will perform many mighty miracles in the lives of His children. [**M.E. Smoot, *Ensign*, Nov. 2000, 89–92**] As you exercise your priesthood, in righteousness [**D&C 121:39–46**], you will see the hand of the Lord manifest; and your testimony of the reality of God and His power will deepen and increase. I bless you that your tongue will be loosed [**D&C 11:21, 31:3**] as you speak on behalf of the Lord, so that your words will be His words, and the promises you make in His name He will justify. [**D&C 132:59; Moses 6:34**] Indeed, as you act as the voice during the numerous priesthood blessings that you will be privileged to pronounce, you—and those you bless—will sense the thinness of the veil [***Teachings of the Prophet Joseph Smith*, 325**] and the reality of modern-day revelation. One of the strongest components of your testimony will be the reality that the priesthood is real. Because of this great blessing that God has bestowed upon you, ever express gratitude to your Heavenly Father for the sacred opportunity He has given you to hold and exercise His power. [**D&C 59:21**]

I know of some who have actually penciled into the margins of their blessing the dates of when they feel certain parts of it were (at least partially) fulfilled.

Many people have found various ways to analyze their blessing, looking for promises, gifts, admonitions, and warnings. One source suggested we should carefully write down each of these elements mentioned in our blessing and then record in our journal or in the margins of our blessing any actions we feel the Spirit is prompting us to take.[23] "Remember the specific warnings [given in your blessing]. Put up little notes or reminders where you can see them every day."[24] For some, it might be helpful to create a chart of blessings and admonitions. One source suggested, "Almost every sentence in your patriarchal blessing falls into the category of a blessing or an admonition."[25] Creating a chart like the ones below—and tying certain blessings to their associated admonitions—can be a helpful way to bring clarity to what your blessing is saying.[26]

Blessings	Admonitions

Here is another type of chart you might find useful:

Gifts	Promises	Counsel	Warnings

I liked the wise counsel given by one stake patriarch. He suggested that, as you read your scriptures each day, you take out your blessing and ask yourself, "Based on what my patriarchal blessing says about me and my life's mission, how do these things the Lord and His prophets have taught apply to me?"[27] This is a great way to make your daily scripture study more applicable to your life.

If you are single, when you are dating, read your blessing

often—looking for things it says about your future spouse. Compare those things to the people you are dating. "After pondering her blessing, [one] young woman admitted the young man she was dating didn't match the description of her husband given in it. This realization helped her to break up with him."[28]

As a husband or wife, you should read your spouse's blessing with some frequency. When two people merge their lives (through marriage), their blessings heavily intertwine. Much of what is promised to your spouse in his or her blessing now pertains to you. Therefore, you should use their blessing to better understand what the Lord wants of the two of you. Reading your spouse's blessing can also help to strengthen the relationship between the two of you. It can help you to see your spouse as the Lord sees him or her. In addition, it can even help you to look past their weaknesses. As an example, one sister noted:

> I had been feeling disgusted with the slow progress my husband was making spiritually while feeling smugly superior in my own diligence. After reading his blessing, I was overcome with its beauty and promises. The number of gifts mentioned and the Lord's obvious confidence in this man to use the difficult experiences of his life in positive ways brought tears to my eyes. . . . I read him some of the things I had underlined in his blessing and expressed my love for him. The tone in our home changed markedly, and I was humbled to remember how different the Lord's perspective is from ours. I needed to repent of my self-righteousness.[29]

Prayerfully read your spouse's blessing with some frequency, and seek the Spirit's promptings as you do so.

Similarly, if you are a parent, read your children's patriarchal blessings often so that, when you counsel them, you will have in mind the things the Lord has revealed about them—and also the things He has warned them about. For example, one father holds monthly personal priesthood interviews with his children, but he rereads their blessings prior to doing so and then uses what he has read in their patriarchal blessings to know what to ask them about, or what to counsel them on.[30]

Of course, you should use your blessing to test some of the

messages of the world, thereby making sure that you are not being led astray. Let it provide you hope and confidence in those times when you need it the most. Sister Julie B. Beck (b. 1954), fifteenth General President of the Relief Society, shared an experience of how her patriarchal blessing helped her when she felt discouraged:

> When I was in high school, a counselor read the results of my test scores and told me she did not think I would do well in college. But after I prayerfully studied my patriarchal blessing, I felt I should not abandon my lifelong goal. So, because I had insight into the Lord's plan for me, I had hope in my heart, and I was able to move ahead confidently. I discovered that I was successful in that setting, and I earned a university diploma. When we know who we are and what we are supposed to do, it is easier to make important decisions about education, careers, and marriage. It is easier to shine our light in our families, with our friends, and in all other places.[31]

Your blessing will foresee some of the false messages that will be given to you during your lifetime. If you know your blessing well (through thoughtfully studying it), the Spirit will bring lines from your patriarchal blessing to your mind in those dark hours in which Satan is trying to discourage you by sending you false messages. In those times, your blessing can be a remarkable strength.

One author suggested, "Some people are disappointed because they believe the promises in their blessings are all fulfilled and there is nothing left to look forward to." Of course, "such disappointment is based on [a] misconception."[32] For example, if your blessing says that you will serve a mission—and you did that at eighteen or nineteen years of age—does that mean that this part of your blessing is fulfilled, and that you'll never serve again? Of course not. What if your blessing says you'll have the gift of tongues or the gift of healing? Will that be a one-time manifestation of that gift? Of course not. What if your blessing says you'll be called upon to serve others? Could it not be a life-long mission for you to serve and bless others? None of our patriarchal blessings is so narrow that we can completely fulfill everything mentioned in them during this lifetime. Some things won't be fulfilled until the next life, and other promises will be fulfilled over and over again throughout our life.

In order to make the most of your blessing, don't write things off. Don't assume, once you've experienced them, that you can't experience them again. Seek to bring to pass the Lord's promises to you over and over again.

Finally, I've offered lots of suggestions in this section as to how you might productively use your blessing. Remember, however, you don't need to do *all* of these. Pick one or two of the suggestions I have made and try them for a while. They might help you to better understand, love, and fulfill your blessing. After you've tried for a time one or two of the suggestions I've given, try others. These too may prove helpful to you. If you do too many at once, you'll not do any well. You have a long life ahead of you. Make the pursuit of better understanding and living your blessing a life-long quest.

Notes

1. Brigham Young, in *Journal of Discourses*, 8:55.
2. See Gordon B. Hinckley, *Teachings of Gordon B. Hinckley* (Salt Lake City, UT: Deseret Book, 1997), 422–23.
3. Joseph Fielding Smith, "Address of Joseph Fielding Smith," Advanced Theology, Church History and Philosophy 245 course lecture, June 15, 1956, 8.
4. Garry H. Boyle, *A Loving Letter from God: Your Patriarchal Blessing* (Springville, UT: Cedar Fort, 2015), 67.
5. Thomas S. Monson, "Your Patriarchal Blessing: A Liahona of Light," *Ensign*, November 1986, 66.
6. Boyle, *A Loving Letter from God*, 19.
7. Ed J. Pinegar and Richard J. Allen, *Your Patriarchal Blessing* (American Fork, UT: Covenant Communications, 2005), 87.
8. Bruce E. Dana, *The Apostleship* (Springville, UT: Cedar Fort, 2006), 136–138.
9. Lester J. Petersen, *Your Patriarchal Blessing and the Extraordinary You* (Rexburg, ID: Self-published, 1997), 51.
10. Pinegar and Allen, *Your Patriarchal Blessing*, 49.
11. See Gayla Wise, *The Power of Your Patriarchal Blessing* (Provo, UT: Spring Creek, 2007), 90.
12. Pinegar and Allen, *Your Patriarchal Blessing*, 46.
13. Boyle, *A Loving Letter from God*, 20.
14. Ezra Taft Benson, "Jesus Christ—Gifts and Expectations," *Ensign*, December 1988, 4.
15. Hyrum G. Smith, *Conference Report*. April 1924, 89.

16. John A. Widtsoe, *Evidences and Reconciliations*, vol. 1 (Salt Lake City, UT: Bookcraft, 1943), 76.

17. See Boyle, *A Loving Letter from God*, 13.

18. See John L. Lund, *Understanding Your Patriarchal Blessing* (Orem, UT: Noble Publishing, 1980), preface.

19. Boyle, *A Loving Letter from God*, 55.

20. See Lund, *Understanding Your Patriarchal Blessing*, 21.

21. Lund, 26–27.

22. See Pinegar and Allen, *Your Patriarchal Blessing*, 44.

23. See Pinegar and Allen, 44, 48.

24. Pinegar and Allen, 75.

25. Lund, *Understanding Your Patriarchal Blessing*, 18.

26. For examples of charts, see Lund, *Understanding Your Patriarchal Blessing*, 18. See also Wise, *The Power of Your Patriarchal Blessing*, 93.

27. See Lester J. Petersen, *Your Patriarchal Blessing and the Extraordinary You* (Rexburg, ID: Self-published, 1997), 11–12.

28. Wise, *The Power of Your Patriarchal Blessing*, 124.

29. Wise, 137–138.

30. See Wise, 137.

31. Julie B. Beck, "You Have a Noble Birthright," *Ensign*, May 2006, 107.

32. Wise, *The Power of Your Patriarchal Blessing*, 105.

—54—

How Do I Interpret
My Patriarchal Blessing?

YOUR PATRIARCHAL BLESSING WAS GIVEN BY THE SPIRIT; THERE-fore, it must be interpreted by the Spirit. One of the responsibilities of the Holy Ghost is to teach of truth and to testify of truth. Consequently, understanding and interpreting your blessing is a "spiritual process."[1] If you'll keep the Spirit with you and pray for its guidance each time you read your blessing, you will receive personal revelation as to what it means for the stage of life you're currently in. The only way to rightly interpret and apply your blessing is through the influence of the Holy Ghost.

Sometimes members are tempted to ask others that they respect to help them interpret their blessing. President Boyd K. Packer (1924–2015), former president of the Quorum of the Twelve Apostles, cautioned us not to "ask others to interpret it. Neither the patriarch nor the bishop can or should interpret it."[2] It is our duty—and ours alone—to seek out, by revelation, the meaning of our blessing. This is one reason why we should make sure we are developing spiritual maturity before we receive our blessing: it will take spiritual *work* to understand it once the blessing has been pronounced.

One stake patriarch made an interesting suggestion regarding how members might best interpret their patriarchal blessings. He explained, "Blessings are feelings. Read [your patriarchal blessing] for feelings rather than words. Blessings carry the Spirit. . . . A scripture says that when a man speaketh by the Holy Ghost, the Holy Ghost carries it to the heart of men. (See 2 Ne. 33:1.) So, if you have [a] clean heart and hands when you read it, a powerful Spirit goes with it."[3] Another stake patriarch I am acquainted with said, "I don't have the vocabulary to express exactly what God shows me when I place my hands upon someone's head. So, the meaning of the blessing will be found less in the exact words spoken and more in the feelings that accompany those words." Simply put, you should look for the feelings and promptings you have when you read your blessing. Record those and follow them promptly. As stated earlier, patriarchal blessings are "lightning rods for new revelation."[4] Thus, the feelings you have when you read yours are of sacred importance and should be heeded.

One additional caution about interpreting your blessing is worth mentioning. Don't limit the meaning of your blessing. What you think it means today my only be part of what the Lord is trying to tell you through it. President Gordon B. Hinckley (1910–2008), fifteenth President of the Church, shared the following, which illustrates this principle:

> I received a patriarchal blessing when I was a boy. In that blessing it said that I would lift my voice in testimony of the truth in the nations of the earth. I had labored in London for a long time and given my testimony many times there. We came here [to Amsterdam], and I had opportunity in a meeting to say a few words and offer my testimony. We then went to Berlin, where I had a similar opportunity. We then went to Paris, where I had a similar opportunity. We then went to the United States, to Washington, D.C., and on a Sunday there I had a similar opportunity. When I arrived home, I was tired. . . . I said, "I . . . have completed [that] phase of my blessing. I have lifted my voice in the great capitals of the world—in London, Berlin, Paris, and Washington." And I really felt that way. But somehow, under the providence of the Lord, I have been blessed to lift my voice in scores of nations and lands where the word of the Lord, the restored gospel, has been carried forth.[5]

Similarly, President James E. Faust (1920–2007), a counselor to President Hinckley, shared a promise from his father's patriarchal blessing, which turned out to be fulfilled in a way other than expected:

150

[President Faust's father] was told in his blessing that he would be blessed with "many beautiful daughters." He and my mother became the parents of five sons. No daughters were born to them, but they treated the wives of their sons as daughters. Some years ago when we had a family gathering, I saw my father's daughters-in-law, granddaughters, and great-granddaughters moving about, tending to the food and ministering to the young children and the elderly, and the realization came to me that Father's blessing literally had been fulfilled. He has indeed many beautiful daughters. The patriarch who gave my father his blessing had spiritual vision to see beyond this life. The dividing line between time and eternity disappeared.[6]

By reading into our blessing an interpretation that is incorrect, we can miss what the Lord is actually trying to tell us—and perhaps bring some measure of frustration or heartache. For example, if you see things in your blessing that seem wrong to you—such as being told that you come from "goodly" parents, when your parents have been unkind or unrighteous—do not assume that the patriarch has been uninspired or somehow made a mistake. Seek, through the Spirit, to know what the Lord meant by that. It is quite possible that He was speaking of your parental ancestors; they may have been "goodly" even though your mother and father have struggled. On the other hand, perhaps your "goodly" parentage is a reference to the fact that you are literally of the blood of Israel, and your father of the covenant—Abraham—was certainly "goodly." Of course, you know that your Heavenly Parents are "goodly" in every sense of the word. Perhaps the declaration of your parents' "goodliness" is a statement about things your mortal mother and father have done for you or provided you with that you have taken for granted. My point is, don't assume—when you see something you disagree with or don't understand—that the patriarch was uninspired. Instead, prayerfully ask the Lord to reveal to you what that part of your blessing means.[7] Elder Eldred G. Smith (1907–2013), the last general Patriarch to the Church, indicated that most of our blessings will make promises— or speak of things—that we simply will not understand when we first get the blessing. However, "through continued faith, the time will come when the interpretation will be given to us."[8] Thus, as you prayerfully read and ponder your blessing over the span of your life, leave open the possibility of the Lord revealing to you meanings you did not see when you first received your blessing.

Notes

1. Ed J. Pinegar and Richard J. Allen, *Your Patriarchal Blessing* (American Fork, UT: Covenant Communications, 2005), 39, 40.
2. Boyd K. Packer, "The Stake Patriarch," *Ensign*, November 2002, 43.
3. See Gayla Wise, *The Power of Your Patriarchal Blessing* (Provo, UT: Spring Creek, 2007), 86.
4. Garry H. Boyle, *A Loving Letter from God: Your Patriarchal Blessing* (Springville, UT: Cedar Fort, 2015), 111.
5. Gordon B. Hinckley, "Amsterdam, Netherlands, Missionary Meeting," June 13, 1996, in *Discourses of President Gordon B. Hinckley, Volume 1: 1995–1999* (Salt Lake City, UT: The Church of Jesus Christ of Latter-day Saints, 2004), 426.
6. James E. Faust, "Priesthood Blessings," *Ensign*, November 1995, 83.
7. See Boyle, *A Loving Letter from God*, 161–162; Wise, *The Power of Your Patriarchal Blessing*, 100–101.
8. Eldred G. Smith, "What Is a Patriarchal Blessing?" *The Instructor* 97, no. 2 (February 1962): 43.

—55—

Why Do Some People Say That the Meaning of Their Blessing Has Changed over Time?

It has been said that "each time you read your blessing, you will see different things. You will perceive a different emphasis at different times in your life. What you perceive in reading your blessing when you are a teenager may be different from what you perceive when you are a missionary or a mother or father. In other words, as you occupy different roles in your life, you will come to view blessings in ways that apply to you at that time."[1] I don't know that you'll necessarily see different things "each time you read your blessing." Nevertheless, it is *absolutely* the case that, as you mature and as your life circumstances change, passages that meant one thing to you at one stage will take on an entirely different meaning during a later stage of your life. In this regard, your patriarchal blessing is like any other passage of scripture. This is one reason why it is so important for you to read and reread your blessing often.

Over time—"line upon line, precept upon precept"—God will reveal to you the meaning and significance of your patriarchal blessing (2 Nephi 28:30).[2] President James E. Faust (1920–2007), a member of the First Presidency, spoke of how he and his wife read their patriarchal blessings together when he was eighty-three years old. After reading them, he said, "We found we still have additional work to do."[3] How could this be? How could there be things talked about in his blessing that he only noticed at eighty-three years of age? Father in Heaven knows when you are ready to understand a certain phrase, promise, or advice given in your blessing. He will reveal those things when it is best for you—*and not before.*[4] One patriarch suggested, "Though the words of your blessing will remain the same, your understanding of the meaning and the ideas will change in accordance with the circumstances in your life."[5] Thus, like many who have come before you, one day you will be reading in your blessing—a blessing you have read many times before—and a line or phrase will jump out at you, and you will say to yourself, "I've never noticed that before." This is one reason why patriarchal blessings can be described as "a gift that keeps on giving."

Notes

1. Ed J. Pinegar and Richard J. Allen, *Your Patriarchal Blessing* (American Fork, UT: Covenant Communications, 2005), 42.
2. See Garry H. Boyle, *A Loving Letter from God: Your Patriarchal Blessing* (Springville, UT: Cedar Fort, 2015), 71.
3. James E. Faust, "Challenges Facing the Family," *Worldwide Leadership Training Meeting*, January 10, 2004, 2.
4. See Gayla Wise, *The Power of Your Patriarchal Blessing* (Provo, UT: Spring Creek, 2007), 93.
5. Lester J. Petersen, *Your Patriarchal Blessing and the Extraordinary You* (Rexburg, ID: Self-published, 1997), 37, 43.

—56—

How Will Regularly Reading and Thinking about My Patriarchal Blessing Influence My Testimony?

A PATRIARCHAL BLESSING IS PROOF THAT HEAVENLY FATHER KNOWS you *by name* and that He is intimately aware of you. It shows that, in addition to the plan of salvation—which is for *all* of His children— He also has a plan *specifically for you* and your life.[1] If you regularly read your blessing and contemplate its promises, warnings, and counsel, you will notice it being fulfilled throughout your life. When you notice that these prophecies about you are coming to pass, your testimony that the patriarch was inspired will be increased—as will your testimony that God knows and loves you. Your blessing, if you use it regularly, will be a great proof to you that there is a God, and that His Church is true. If you ever wonder, "Does Heavenly Father love me?" read your blessing and you'll know that He does and that He has great blessings in store for you as one of His children.

Anxiety and self-doubt are common—particularly in these latter-days. There are incredible pressures bearing down on people, pressures unique to this time in the history of the world. While your parents and grandparents probably had to work harder physically than you do, your generation has more social pressures and temptations than previous ones. The emotional and spiritual work required to stay spiritually healthy is more than it used to be. Consequently, many who have struggled with sins or what they perceive as a lack of personal accomplishment tend to think poorly of themselves. However, if you read your patriarchal blessing through—looking for the good qualities that it says you have or that you are blessed with—you will see yourself the way your Father in Heaven sees you. What the world says of you is often a lie. However, what your Father in Heaven sees in you is the truth. What your patriarchal blessing describes is *the real you!*[2]

One author suggested that you should "make it a practice to talk about the influence of your own blessing in your life over the years."[3] While we should not go into detail with just anyone about all of the promises made in our blessings, nevertheless, it seems fair to say that, as we testify to others of our blessing's inspired nature, not only will our own testimony of its inspiration grow, but others will also have their faith in the inspired nature of patriarchal blessings strengthened. Parents should pay particular attention to this counsel. A wise parent will look for opportunities to testify to his or her children about the inspired nature of their blessing, as this will inspire their children to want a blessing also.

There is value in recording in your journal both the things you felt the day you received your blessing and also any experiences you have throughout your life that evidence that your blessing is being fulfilled. (It may be helpful to record these in the same place—perhaps on some paper that you keep with your blessing.) You may also wish to record other personal revelations you receive in this same location. That will help you to have a "repository," of sorts, of God's instructions to you and a record of how He fulfilled those revelations and promises. This will be a blessing to you, but it will also help your children and grandchildren once you have passed.

The question has been asked, "How often should I read my blessing?" One patriarch responded, "How often should you read the scriptures?"[4] Because a patriarchal blessing is personal scripture, you should read it, ponder it, and study it often. While you may not choose to read it every day, reading it monthly would certainly not be too frequent.

Notes

1. See Ed J. Pinegar and Richard J. Allen, *Your Patriarchal Blessing* (American Fork, UT: Covenant Communications, 2005), 5.
2. See Gayla Wise, *The Power of Your Patriarchal Blessing* (Provo, UT: Spring Creek, 2007), 89.
3. Grant Von Harrison, *Fathers as Patriarchs* (Sandy, UT: Sounds of Zion, 1990), 56.
4. See Wise, *The Power of Your Patriarchal Blessing*, 20.

—57—

Is Keeping the Commandments Sufficient to Realize All of the Blessings Promised to Me?

THE OFT-REPEATED COLLOQUIALISM IS TRUE, "IF YOU FAIL TO PLAN, you plan to fail." The promises made to you in a patriarchal blessing will *not* come to pass if you idly sit by waiting for the Lord to bless you. You must do your part. You must work to bring them to pass. You must make plans to make them a reality in your life. Elder John A. Widtsoe (1872–1952) of the Quorum of the Twelve Apostles suggested that we must do more than just *be good*. We must *work* for our blessings. "They must be earned," he said. "The patriarch only indicates the gifts the Lord would give us, if we labor for them. He helps us by pointing out the divine goal which we may enjoy if we pay the price."[1] One stake patriarch pointed out, "What we get out of our blessing depends on what we do to help Heavenly Father continue to bless us."[2] In Moroni 10:8, we are commanded to "deny not the gifts of God." We deny them when we don't seek after them or work for them. Consequently, you should periodically read your blessing with this question in mind: "Is there anything I need to change in my life in order to fulfill the promises made to me in my patriarchal blessing?"[3]

When you were confirmed a member of The Church of Jesus Christ of Latter-day Saints, priesthood holders placed their hands upon your head and commanded you to "receive the Holy Ghost." We often say in the Church that "receiving the Holy Ghost" is different from being "given" the Holy Ghost. To *receive* implies you must do something. Just as you must live so as to be worthy to *receive* the Spirit in your life, you too must act in order to *receive* the blessings pronounced upon you in your patriarchal blessing. One patriarch explained, "Just because your blessing says [or promises you] something does not mean that it will happen without your involvement."[4] We must actively seek to be a partner with God in bringing to pass the promises made in our blessing. For example, if it says you'll serve a full-time mission, you have to make that happen. If it says you'll marry in the temple, you have to make that happen. If we lose the Spirit by not living worthily, we can repent and regain its companionship and blessings. Similarly, if we are living in such a way as to negate some of the promises in our patriarchal blessing, we should repent and turn to Christ so that we can again be worthy of the things promised to us therein.

Notes

1. John A. Widtsoe, *Evidences and Reconciliations*, vol. 1 (Salt Lake City, UT: Bookcraft, 1943), 74–75.
2. Lester J. Petersen, *Your Patriarchal Blessing and the Extraordinary You* (Rexburg, ID: Self-published, 1997), 16.
3. See Petersen, *Your Patriarchal Blessing and the Extraordinary You*, 38.
4. Garry H. Boyle, *A Loving Letter from God: Your Patriarchal Blessing* (Springville, UT: Cedar Fort, 2015), 10.

—58—

What Is Meant by the Promise That I Will Come Forth in the Morning of the First Resurrection?

ELDER BRUCE R. McCONKIE (1915–1985) OF THE QUORUM OF THE Twelve Apostles wrote, "Nothing is more absolutely universal than the Resurrection."[1] Though all people will be resurrected (1 Corinthians 15:22), not all will be resurrected at the same time. Technically speaking, there are four resurrections.

The Morning of the First Resurrection: This resurrection began with Christ's Resurrection and will continue in and through the Millennium. This resurrection is reserved for those who have lived righteously. It is reserved for those who are destined to be heirs of the celestial kingdom.

The Afternoon of the First Resurrection: This resurrection starts once the Millennium has begun and will carry on throughout the thousand years of the Millennium. It is reserved for those who have lived good lives but were not necessarily valiant. This resurrection is reserved for those who are destined to inherit the terrestrial kingdom.

The Morning of the Second Resurrection: This resurrection begins at the end of the Millennium. It is reserved for those who have lived sinful lives, for those who have lived contrary to the dictates for their conscience and the promptings of the Holy Spirit. Those who come forth in this resurrection will inherit the telestial kingdom, the lowest of the three degrees of glory. Those who inherit this glory will not spend eternity in the presence of Satan and his minions. However, they will be eternally shut out of the presence of God and Christ.

The Afternoon of the Second Resurrection: This resurrection will take place after all others have been resurrected. It is reserved for the sons and daughters[2] of perdition, for those who will spend eternity with the devil and his angels because, in mortality, they did the work of the devil and his angels. It is the only of the four resurrections that provides its recipients with *no glory whatsoever.* Hence, the eternal abode for those who come forth in this resurrection is known as "outer darkness" (Alma 40:13), where God's light *never* shines (D&C 88:6–13).

Thus, what does it mean if your patriarchal blessing promises you that you will "come forth in the morning of the First Resurrection"? One stake patriarch I am acquainted with suggested that it means you will be resurrected "at the first opportunity you are able to be." It certainly means that if you are true to your covenants, you will be exalted. It is the promise that, through your faithfulness and through Christ's Atonement, you are going to make it to the celestial kingdom, where you will preside over your posterity for eternity, doing what God does, because you will have become what He is. Could there be any greater promise that God could make to any of His children?

Notes

1. John A. Widtsoe, *Evidences and Reconciliations*, vol. 1 (Salt Lake City, UT: Bookcraft, 1943), 74–75.
2. Lester J. Petersen, *Your Patriarchal Blessing and the Extraordinary You* (Rexburg, ID: Self-published, 1997), 16.
3. See Petersen, *Your Patriarchal Blessing and the Extraordinary You*, 38.
4. Garry H. Boyle, *A Loving Letter from God: Your Patriarchal Blessing* (Springville, UT: Cedar Fort, 2015), 10.

—59—

Why Did God Mention Certain Gifts of the Spirit in My Patriarchal Blessing?

Elder Marvin J. Ashton (1915–1994), who served as a member of the Quorum of the Twelve Apostles, taught that there are many gifts of the Spirit, some of which we may not think are actually spiritual endowments. Among others, he mentioned the following:

> The gift of asking; the gift of listening; the gift of hearing and using a still, small voice; the gift of being able to weep; the gift of avoiding contention; the gift of being agreeable; the gift of avoiding vain repetition; the gift of seeking that which is righteous; the gift of not passing judgment; the gift of looking to God for guidance; the gift of being a disciple; the gift of caring for others; the gift of being able to ponder; the gift of offering prayer; the gift of bearing a mighty testimony; and the gift of receiving the Holy Ghost.[1]

Elder Ashton added to his list other less-known gifts of the Spirit, such as the gift to ponder, the gift of looking to God for direction, the gift to calm others, and the gift to care.[2] Elder Bruce R. McConkie (1915–1985), also a member of the Quorum of the Twelve Apostles, said of the various gifts of the Spirit, "In the fullest sense, they are infinite in number and endless in their manifestations."[3] Both Elder Ashton and Elder McConkie were suggesting that there are many different types of gifts that the Holy Ghost can endow you with—and which may be mentioned in your patriarchal blessing. Your gifts may be very different from those of your siblings, parents, or friends. Nevertheless, they are all gifts from God, and they all require that we keep the Spirit with us if we wish them to be manifest in our lives.

The gifts of the Spirit mentioned in your blessing can serve as a key to discovering your purpose in life, to realizing what your mortal mission and ministry will be about. Of course, some gifts of the Spirit will help you to avoid sin and temptation. However, others will allow you to be an instrument in God's hands to bless His other children. One patriarch pointed out, "Many gifts are not given for the personal benefit of the individual who has the gifts [promised to them], but rather for that person to use them to bless others. Why? . . . In using gifts to bless others, we are acting like Christ, or in other words, through the process of using gifts to bless others we become Christlike, which is the goal of this life."[4] As you use your various gifts in righteous service, your heart and desires will change, and you will become more like your Savior.[5] Thus, God has mentioned these gifts in your blessing because He knows they will help you to be exalted; they will help you to become like He is—and that will fill your life with power and protection.

Additionally, if you are willing to study the gifts of the Spirit mentioned in your blessing, you will begin to increase in your desire for those gifts. Also, as you study what the scriptures and living prophets have said about the specific gifts you have been promised, you will increase the likelihood that you will experience significant manifestations of those gifts.[6] Of course, being promised a gift doesn't mean you'll necessarily have that gift. You must work to understand and develop the gifts God says you have a right to. Remember, Oliver Cowdery was told by God that he had the gift to translate, but Oliver never took the time to understand and develop that gift. Consequently, he never actually received the gift that God told him he had a right to (D&C 9:7–11). You must do more than simply rejoice in the gifts God has promised you. You must do all within your power to develop them.

Notes

1. See Marvin J. Ashton, "There Are Many Gifts," *Ensign*, November 1987, 20.
2. See Ashton, "There Are Many Gifts," 20–23.

3. Bruce R. McConkie, *Mormon Doctrine*, 2nd ed. (Salt Lake City, UT: Bookcraft, 1979), 314.
4. Garry H. Boyle, *A Loving Letter from God: Your Patriarchal Blessing* (Springville, UT: Cedar Fort, 2015), 105.
5. Boyle, *A Loving Letter from God*, 89.
6. See Boyle, 91.

—60—

What Role Will My Spouse's Blessing Play in My Life?

ONCE YOU ARE ENGAGED TO BE MARRIED, THAT *MAY* BE A GOOD time for you and your fiancé to share your patriarchal blessings with each other as a means of having some sense of your soon-to-be-combined missions. You should certainly read each other's blessings once you are married—and occasionally throughout your married lives. One patriarch suggested that, by reading each other's blessings, "you can help each other stay focused."[1] Elsewhere we read, "Sometimes we gain understanding about ourselves through the patriarchal blessing of one of our family members."[2] (Of course, other than the blessings of your spouse, children, and ancestors, you probably should not be reading other family member's blessings.) Once you marry, your spouse's blessing—*in part*—becomes *your* blessing. One sister said, "When I read my husband's patriarchal blessing, the Spirit told me that it was a completion of my own."[3] Truly, the things promised to the person you are (or will be) sealed to will pertain to you and your life. The plans for his or her life become part of your life. The counsel regarding his or her children pertain to your children. The advice about the education or career he or she received from the Lord have a bearing on your own education and career. Thus, you should read and pray to understand your spouse's blessing and to have the strength to live so that you can fulfill it.

Additionally, if you wish to understand your spouse and really live to serve and bless him or her, studying his or her patriarchal blessing will inspire you to both better understand the person you've married and to see them as God sees them—and serve them as Father in Heaven would want you to serve them.

Notes

1. Garry H. Boyle, *A Loving Letter from God: Your Patriarchal Blessing* (Springville, UT: Cedar Fort, 2015), 111.
2. Gayla Wise, *The Power of Your Patriarchal Blessing* (Provo, UT: Spring Creek, 2007), 111.
3. See Wise, *The Power of Your Patriarchal Blessing*, 111.

—61—

What If My Blessing Isn't Very Long?

PRESIDENT THOMAS S. MONSON (1927–2018) STATED, "LENGTH and language do not a patriarchal blessing make."[1] Each blessing is different, in its style, length, and content. That's one of the reasons why it is special; that's what makes it uniquely yours. Patriarchs are counseled by their leaders to not make the blessings they pronounce extremely long. Indeed, most blessings are between one and two pages in length. For example, President Gordon B. Hinckley's (1910–2008) patriarchal blessing was only one page long. President Heber J. Grant's (1856–1945) patriarchal blessing was only one third of a page. These two men were prophets, seers, and revelators—and they were two of the greatest men to ever live upon the earth—and yet neither of them received a patriarchal blessing that was longer than a page in length. Thus, if your blessing seems short, you're in good company. President James E. Faust (1920–2007), of the First Presidency, said of his patriarchal blessing, "My own blessing is short, and it is limited to perhaps three quarters of a page on one side, yet it has been completely adequate and perfect for me."[2] Your patriarchal blessing is not intended to be a declaration of *all* than can or will happen to you in your life. It is only a sampling of the possibilities that will come, if you are faithful. Brother Karl G. Maeser (1828–1901), the founder of Brigham Young University, explained, "Our Patriarchal Blessings are paragraphs from the book of our possibilities."[3] A "paragraph" is only a snippet of a "book"— and your blessing only contains excerpts from your book of life, though those "excerpts" may be some of the most important ones.

Elder Hyrum G. Smith (1879–1932), general Patriarch to the Church, taught, "I should like to admonish my brethren and sisters . . . not to be easily discouraged and think that because their blessing is short it is incomplete, or because it contains only a few promises, that there is something else that has not been written or has not been promised."[4] Indeed, God knows exactly what you'll need in order to make your way back to His presence. Your patriarchal blessing will contain exactly what it should; no more, no less. As you make the study of your blessing a life-long pursuit, God will reveal to you the equivalent of pages and pages of insights as to what your blessing means and what you need to do. Your blessing is the key by which you can unlock the door to marvelous revelations in your life. Keys are always small, but the treasures they can unlock are enormous!

Notes

1. Thomas S. Monson, "Your Patriarchal Blessing: A Liahona of Light," *Ensign*, November 1986, 66.
2. James E. Faust, "Priesthood Blessings," *Ensign*, November 1995, 82.
3. Karl G. Maeser, quoted in Reed Smoot, in Conference Report, October 1937, 18.
4. Hyrum G. Smith, in Conference Report, April 1921, 185.

—62—

Is It Okay for Me to Read Someone Else's Patriarchal Blessing or to Share Mine with Others?

DURING MY MISSION, I OFTEN HEARD MISSIONARIES TALKING about the content of their patriarchal blessings. Some, I suppose, shared their blessings with their companions. On several occasions, I have myself been asked by someone what I thought a given line or phrase in their blessing meant. While such curiosity may be natural, it is probably best to not share your blessing with friends, nor to read or seek to interpret theirs. Doctrine and Covenants 63:64 states, "Remember that that which cometh from above is sacred, and must be spoken with care, and by constraint of the Spirit." We have been counseled to be careful about who we share our patriarchal blessings with. Elder Eldred G. Smith (1907–2013), general Patriarch to the Church, said, "I do not recommend . . . reading each other's blessings like missionaries do in reading their companion's blessings and students in school reading their roommate's blessings. This I don't recommend because those [individuals] don't have the right of interpreting your blessing. Others could easily misinterpret [it] and misguide [you]."[1] Just as others do not have the right to correctly interpret our patriarchal blessing, we do not have the right to interpret other people's blessings. The Spirit is only going to reveal the meaning of a blessing to the person the blessing belongs to. Consequently, if you are invited to read the blessing of a friend, you should probably politely decline. Were you to read it, your friend would most likely want to know your thoughts an interpretation. In offering your opinion or interpretation, you may misguide your friend by what you say. Thus, it is usually best to not engage in reading each other's blessings and to not offer interpretations of all or part of another person's blessing.

There is another risk associated with reading someone else's blessing. I have known of individuals who have read a friend's blessing and felt that they would have preferred their friend's blessing to their own. A spirit of jealously and dissatisfaction came into their life, and their own blessing became less treasured by them. The Lord has commanded us to not covet (Exodus 20:17). We typically think of coveting as wanting some material item that someone else has that we currently do not. However, it is equally inappropriate to covet the spiritual blessings someone has been promised. Thus, reading another's blessing, can lead to coveting—which is a sin.

Another problem with reading someone else's blessing is that you might notice similarities between their blessing and yours. For some, this may make their own blessing seem less special or less personal. However, you need to remember that the principles of the gospel apply to all of us. Thus, certain statements, and even some promises, are universally applicable—and might appear in *most* patriarchal blessings. For example, many members of the Church will be called upon to serve a full-time mission. Thus, it is common in patriarchal blessings for someone to be told that they were foreordained to serve a mission. Similarly, certain gifts of the Spirit are common to members of the Church—such as the gift of leadership—and, therefore, may be mentioned in many people's blessings. This does not mean that these promises to you are "less special" because they were also made to others. Their appearance in your blessing only goes to show that you have been foreordained by God to do some very important or significant things. Just as there are thousands of missionaries in the Church with very similar callings, God has foreordained thousands of His children to have certain gifts and talents which will be used to build up His kingdom upon the earth in the latter days.

While we are discouraged from reading the patriarchal blessings of friends, roommates, missionary companions, or even siblings,[2] the Brethren have suggested that it *would* be appropriate for you to read the blessing of your spouse and children, in addition to the blessings of your deceased direct-line ancestors.[3] One patriarch indicated that he had read his great-grandfather's blessing, and discovered that he (as the great-grandson) had been part of the fulfillment of that blessing. (You may obtain and read the patriarchal blessings of your deceased ancestors of whom you are a direct descendant.[4]) If your parents are still living and have their own patriarchal blessings, you may also want to ask them if there are things in their patriarchal blessings that pertain to you or the family that they might share with you—as a means of gaining insight into yourself and your life's mission.[5]

If you are tempted to share your blessing with a friend, or invited to read the blessing of an acquaintance, remember that on several occasions—after revealing sacred and important truths or after performing a miracle—Jesus instructed the recipients of His blessings that they should "tell no man" (see Matthew 8:4, 16:20; Mark 7:36, 8:30, 9:9; Luke 5:14, 8:56, 9:21). Your patriarchal blessing is miracle that reveals sacred and important truths about your life and mission. As a sacred and personal revelation from God to you, you should keep it confidential and "tell no man" of the specifics of its content.

Notes

1. Eldred G. Smith, "Lectures in Theology: Last Message Series," Salt Lake Institute of Religion, April 30, 1971, 5.
2. See Gayla Wise, *The Power of Your Patriarchal Blessing* (Provo, UT: Spring Creek, 2007), 82.
3. See Boyd K. Packer, "The Stake Patriarch," *Ensign*, November 2002, 43. See also John L. Lund, *Understanding Your Patriarchal Blessing* (Orem, UT: Noble Publishing, 1980), 10; Gayla Wise, *The Power of Your Patriarchal Blessing* (Provo, UT: Spring Creek, 2007), 23.
4. See "Patriarchal Blessings," Church History Library, May 31, 2017, https://history.lds.org/article/chl-pb. See also R. Clayton Brough and Thomas W. Grassley, *Understanding Patriarchal Blessings* (Springville, UT: Horizon Publishers, 2008), 76; John L. Lund, *Understanding Your Patriarchal Blessing* (Orem, UT: Noble Publishing, 1980), 15.
5. See Wise, *The Power of Your Patriarchal Blessing*, 19.

—63—

What If My Blessing Doesn't Contain Any Extravagant Promises?

IF YOU EXPECT YOUR PATRIARCHAL BLESSING TO MAKE WILD OR unusual promises and predictions, you may be misunderstanding what a patriarchal blessing is. Your patriarchal blessing isn't a fortune cookie, and the patriarch isn't a fortuneteller.[1] The patriarch is a prophet, called to convey God's words and will to you. He is only authorized to pronounce the promises he is prompted by the Holy Ghost to give. Patriarchs are counseled by their leaders to avoid making sensational or extravagant promises in the blessings they pronounce, even if the Spirit shows them rather remarkable things about the blessing's recipient. President Joseph Fielding Smith (1876–1972), tenth President of the Church, explained, "I know of one or two cases . . . where a brother has been blessed by the patriarch and told that he would become a member of the Council of the Twelve [Apostles]. Usually [the patriarchs] don't say that . . . even if the patriarch felt that the chances are [very good] that a man will be called to the leading councils of the Church." President Smith added, "Patriarchs should be very careful in giving their blessings not to make extravagant expressions and to be conservative in what they say."[2] Thus, you should not expect extravagant things to be mentioned in your blessing. Patriarchs generally avoid, for example, talking about things like the timing of the Second Coming when they give a blessing. While the young man or young woman being blessed *may* live to see the second coming of Christ, most patriarchs simply wouldn't mention that in the blessing. President Smith further explained:

> Sometimes the individual receiving the blessing can't understand all that's in it. Maybe it's [just as] well that he can't. . . . There are some things the patriarch may say in a blessing that he has to say rather guardedly. . . . I call your attention to one: . . . one time a father came to me with his son's patriarchal blessing. In it the patriarch had said: 'In a short time you will be called on an important mission.' That's all he said. It was only a few months later when the young man was killed.[3]

Imagine if the patriarch had told the boy exactly what he had seen when giving that blessing. Such news would have been both devastating and paralyzing for the boy. The Lord knows what we can handle and what's best for us to *not* know. Telling the boy to prepare for an important mission was sufficient warning for him to get ready—even though the young man did not know that what he was preparing for was death. The following scenario illustrates what could happen if the patriarch told us too much when giving us our blessing.

> What if . . . your blessing says someday you will be in a plane crash? Since this is avoidable, you decide never to fly. What blessings—of places seen, relatives visited, special occasions enjoyed, time saved, and experience gained—will you lose? Your choices are stymied [by knowing this extravagant detail]. You act from fear rather than faith and courage. Knowing ahead of [time the] adversity [you will experience in mortality] may block your enjoyment of life and impede your progress. . . . We can be grateful for those things in our blessings that are vague for our own good.[4]

There is safety in a blessing that offers counsel, promises, and warnings—but which withholds some of the details surrounding those promises and warnings. One stake patriarch suggested, "Sometimes we want the unusual. Sometimes our expectation is to receive a new revelation never given before. However, if we stop to think about the rewards promised for living the gospel, they are anything but ordinary."[5] Indeed, as one author wisely pointed out, "The content of any patriarchal blessing is of sufficient depth to challenge the thinking of the most profound [person]."[6] If you don't see in your blessing "extravagant" promises or counsel, it may be because you don't understand your blessing—and, most likely, because you have not paid the price to get the revelation necessary to see what it is God is really saying to you through your patriarchal blessing.

The vagueness of certain phrases in your blessing may actually turn out to be a blessing in disguise. Pronouncements that leave the details vague should cause you to seek God more earnestly in prayer in order to understand exactly what those declarations or promises mean.[7]

Finally, remember, if we know all of the details, our tests would not be tests—and our agency would be severely limited. If our lives are largely planned out for us (as an overly detailed patriarchal blessing would suggest they are), how would we use our agency to grow or to make choices?[8] We should be grateful that God gives us the hints and details that He does, without orchestrating every aspect of our lives.

Notes

1. Virginia H. Pearce, "Faith Is the Answer," *Ensign*, May 1994, 93.
2. Joseph Fielding Smith, "Address of Joseph Fielding Smith," Advanced Theology, Church History and Philosophy 245 course lecture. June 15, 1956, 5.
3. Joseph Fielding Smith, "Address of Joseph Fielding Smith," 5.
4. Gayla Wise, *The Power of Your Patriarchal Blessing* (Provo, UT: Spring Creek, 2007), 94.
5. Garry H. Boyle, *A Loving Letter from God: Your Patriarchal Blessing* (Springville, UT: Cedar Fort, 2015), 56.
6. John L. Lund, *Understanding Your Patriarchal Blessing* (Orem, UT: Noble Publishing, 1980), preface.
7. See Wise, *The Power of Your Patriarchal Blessing*, 97.
8. Boyle, *A Loving Letter from God*, 119.

—64—

How Much Credence Should I Put in Things I Hear Have Been Said in Other People's Patriarchal Blessings?

PRESIDENT HAROLD B. LEE (1899–1973), THE ELEVENTH PRESIDENT of the Church, spoke of his frustration with members of the Church spreading rumors about supposed promises made in patriarchal blessings—promises about the timing of the Second Coming and similar extravagant claims. He noted, "It never ceases to amaze me how gullible some of our Church members are in broadcasting sensational . . . purported patriarchal blessings. . . . One of our brethren is supposed to have had a patriarchal blessing saying he would preside over the Church when the Savior came. This is, of course, false."[1]

A patriarchal blessing is a personal revelation for the recipient—and the recipient *only*. Thus, even if such extravagant claims appeared in someone's blessing—and usually they *do not*—those promises would be for the recipient of the blessing, and him or her *alone*.[2] Therefore, when we hear of such strange or extravagant promises, we should not concern ourselves with them. In most cases, they are not actually true. Regardless, they are *not for us*—or the Lord would have made such promises in our own patriarchal blessing. Satan uses such rumors in an effort to keep you and me from focusing on the things that matter most.

Notes

1. Harold B. Lee, *The Teachings of Harold B. Lee*, Clyde J. Williams, comp. (Salt Lake City, UT: Bookcraft, 1998), 399–400.
2. Thomas S. Monson, "Your Patriarchal Blessing: A Liahona of Light," *Ensign*, November 1986, 66.

—65—

Why Is a Copy of My Blessing Sent to Church Headquarters?

AFTER YOUR BLESSING HAS BEEN TYPED UP, THE PATRIARCH WILL make two copies: one for you and one to be sent (electronically) to the Church Historical Department in Salt Lake City, Utah. The Historical Department of the Church keeps a digital copy of all patriarchal blessings. Thus, your patriarchal blessing is the only personal priesthood blessing you will ever receive in this life of which a word-for-word transcript will be retained in the archives of the Church.[1] When the Apostle John saw in vision the Judgment Day, one of the things he noted was this: "And I saw the dead, small and great, stand before God; and the books were opened: and another book was opened, which is the book of life: and the dead were judged out of those things which were written in the books, according to their works" (Revelation 20:12). It has been suggested that your patriarchal blessing is one of those records placed in the "book of life" from which you will be judged when you stand before the throne of God at the Judgment Day.[2] While that might seem like a scary thought, what a blessing to have the answers to the test way in advance! If you live up to the counsel and commands you receive in your patriarchal blessing, the Judgment Day will be a piece of cake!

Another reason for having a copy of your blessing in the archives of the Church is that, should you lose your copy, you can contact the Church and obtain another copy. (If you lose the written copy within the first twelve months after you received your blessing or if it has somehow been destroyed, you can contact the patriarch who gave you the blessing and he can print out another copy. If it has been more than a year since you received your blessing, you will need to sign onto your LDS.org account in order to request a copy—or write the Church Historical Department directly.)

Notes

1. R. Clayton Brough and Thomas W. Grassley, *Understanding Patriarchal Blessings* (Springville, UT: Horizon Publishers, 2008), 76.
2. Beverly J. Norton, "Record Keeping," in *The Encyclopedia of Mormonism*, Daniel H. Ludlow, ed., 4 vols. (New York: Macmillan Publishers, 1992), 3:1195–1196.

—EPILOGUE—

ONE OF THE REMARKABLE MIRACLES OF OUR DAY IS THE OPPORTUnity to receive a patriarchal blessing. There is a God in His heavens who is literally our Father and who knows us individually; He hears and answers our prayers. Our Heavenly Father has instructed his prophets to authorize the ordination of good and honorable men to the office of patriarch that, through that office and its associated authority, those mere mortals might receive personal revelations on behalf of you and me. In the words of President Gordon B. Hinckley (1910–2008), "What a blessing to receive a patriarchal blessing!"[1] If you will prayerfully and regularly read your patriarchal blessing and faithfully follow its counsel, I promise you—in the name of the Lord—God will pour out upon you rich and abundant blessings, blessings which will ultimately lead you back to dwell eternally in the presence of God. May you ever cherish this most remarkable gift given to you from your loving Father in Heaven.

Note

1. Gordon B. Hinckley, *Teachings of Gordon B. Hinckley* (Salt Lake City, UT: Deseret Book, 1997), 423.

—ABOUT THE AUTHOR—

BROTHER GASKILL WAS REARED NEAR INDEPENDENCE, MISSOURI, where he converted to The Church of Jesus Christ of Latter-day Saints in November 1984. Prior to his conversion, he was a practicing Greek Orthodox. One year after his baptism, he served a full-time mission in England.

Professionally, Brother Gaskill taught seminary for four years in southeastern Idaho, after which he was an institute director at Stanford University and at UC Berkeley. He is currently a professor of Church history and doctrine at Brigham Young University, where his primary teaching focus is world religions and Christian history.

He is the author of numerous articles and books, including

- *Converted: True Mormon Conversion Stories from 15 Religions*
- *Know Your Religions Volume 3: A Comparative Look at Mormonism and Jehovah's Witnesses*

- *Temple Reflections: Insights into the House of the Lord*
- *Catholic and Mormon: A Theological Conversation*
- *Miracles of the Book of Mormon: A Guide to the Symbolic Messages*
- *Miracles of the New Testament: A Guide to the Symbolic Messages*
- *Miracles of the Old Testament: A Guide to the Symbolic Messages*
- *Remember: Sacred Truths We Must Never Forget*
- *The Lost Teachings of Jesus on the Sacred Place of Women*
- *Love at Home: Insights from the Lives of Latter-day Prophets*
- *The Truth about Eden: Understanding the Fall and Our Temple Experience*
- *Odds Are, You're Going to be Exalted: Evidence That the Plan of Salvation Works*
- *The Nativity: Rediscover the Most Important Birth in All History*
- *The Savior and the Serpent: Unlocking the Doctrine of the Fall*
- *The Lost Language of Symbolism: An Essential Aid for Recognizing and Interpreting the Symbols of the Scriptures and the Temple*
- *Our Savior's Love: Hope & Healing in Christ*

He and his wife, Lori, are the parents of five children and reside in Payson, Utah.

Scan to visit

alonzogaskill.wordpress.com